MOSAIC

ALSO BY LOUIS NELSON

Elements of Design
Rowena Reed Kostellow and
The Structure of Visual Relationships
By Gail Greet Hannah   Produced by Louis Nelson

*A Guideline of Interior Design Standards
for Bell System Operator Offices*
AT&T Operations and Engineering Departments
Proprietary

IBM Editorial Guidelines Design Chapter
Proprietary

IN PRAISE OF MOSAIC

Louis Nelson is as eloquent and heartful a scholar and writer about memorials to our nation's wars as he is a masterful designer of one of the most evocative: the Korean War Memorial. The honoring of history; a sense of humanity, courage, sacrifice, united resolve—all the qualities we Americans have been proud to bear—resonate through these memorials, as they do through Louis's words about them. We sorely need this beautiful book—this verbal and pictorial homage—at this, now, the most challenging moment in our nation's history. Thank you, Louis Nelson, for reminding us of what we must continue to be.
    —**John Kelly,** author of *The Great Mortality* and *The Graves Are Walking;* and **Sheila Weller,** author of *Carrie Fisher: A Life on the Edge* and *Girls Like Us: Carole King, Joni Mitchell, Carly Simon*—and the *Journey of a Generation.*

Louis Nelson has written a memorable book—one aptly named Mosaic, one imagines, for the many pieces he has collected that found design expression in his rendering of the Korean War Memorial. Memorials can have a mysterious magic that are capable of changing how we see the world. "Blood and beauty" resides in our national memory he says—but there is also a substance Nelson brings to this forgotten war, an urgent power that is so articulately expressed in this book.
    —**Susan Eisenhower.** Cofounder and Chairman Emerita of the Eisenhower Institute

"Mosaic" is a book with dimension and depth. It is a memoir of the Korean War by one who fought it at another time and place. The book traces the personal and professional development of a major figure in the field of America design. And it is a meditation on this place of monuments in our lives from the artist who designed and built the wall and mural at the Korean War Veterans Memorial in Washington DC.
    —**The Right Reverend Clifton Daniel III**
    Dean, The Cathedral Church of Saint John the Divine

I was enormously moved by MOSAIC. I hope this blurb will help others to find it:
  "How do you create a monument for a war as ambiguous as the Korean War? Louis Nelson was given this difficult job. How it changed him and how it changed its spectators is a story he tells in MOSAIC, recounting his experience turning life and death into design. How wonderful to have his beautifully told story."

—Erica Jong.
Author, Poet

Dear Louis,
I've spent an extremely rewarding day reading Mosaic. The pleasure I've taken in each of my visits to the Memorial, the emotional impact I've experienced, has been amplified by your book, a brilliant piece of work. Its title is spot-on: the cultural imagery of the Korean War is splintered, a series of fragments that fail to capture its consequence. You've brought cohesion to those disparate pieces. You've identified—and conveyed—the patterns that animate them. You've done so through contextualization, the frame that holds the pieces of your mosaic in place: U. S. history—cultural, social, political, military—rendered with deft strokes; a universal history of human conflict beautifully summarized in your Coda; an account of commemorative monuments that resonates against the planning and construction of the Memorial; a richly informative account of the design principles embodied in its creation. You overlay these accounts, brining texture to the Korean War, calling it into being much as the Memorial restores the humanity of those who fought in that conflict. In much the same way that the Wall and its photographs bring ghosts to life, the context that you create re-integrates the Korean War into collective memory. In your words, the Korean Conflict is "at once remembered and also forgotten". For me, the genius of the book inheres in your rendering of both of those polarities.

  Of course, the most important contextualization is the memoir that Mosaic inscribes. Your account of your life, and the relation of that experience to the War and to the Wall, is masterful. The Korean War is a ghostly presence in our histories because our connection to it is remote, impersonal, insubstantial. Your memoir *serves as a ligament that binds us to the War, and illuminates its enduring consequence. You bring the ghosts to life, in other words, by animating them with your memories. At the same time, you foreground memory itself, its evanescence and its power. Memoirs that succeed transcend the narcissistic to achieve something of the universal; personal experience as a lens rather than as a self-portrait. And here, again, you succeed in spades.*

All this and more, my friend. A real achievement. Your friend's daughter's response to the Wall mirrors mine to your narrative. I'm grateful that you shared it with me.

—**William P. Kelly.** The Andrew W. Mellon Director of the Research Libraries, NYPL.

Louis Nelson is a Renaissance Man, creating everything from pantyhose packaging to the Korean War Memorial in Washington, D. C. His mind is fertile. His conversation scintillating. He now has reviewed his life and work in a significant memoir— a book that helps us understand not only his life and work but America's journey during the past decades. A must read.

—**David Black** Scholar-In-Residence. Kirkland House. Harvard University

Mosaic illuminates how war memorials honor both the victims and survivors of war. Louis Nelson tells a moving story of the intersection of personal experience and design in the Korean War memorial. That design provokes our deepest reflections, not only of the past, but of a more peaceful future we can hope for.

Louis Nelson has written an important book that illustrates how the design of the Korean War memorial calls forth our determination to prevent war and work for a more hopeful, peaceful future.

Louis Nelson's Mosaic is a rich tapestry of honest reflection and realistic hope which stimulates us to think deeply about the costs of war and benefits of peace. The thoughtful design of the Korean War memorial expands the meaning of those who sacrificed, who died but also those who live on with traumatic memories.

—**Jonathan F. Fanton.** President Emeritus. American Academy of Arts & Sciences

Louis Nelson's memorial about bringing to granite life the storied history of a memorial to a ghastly war is a memorial in itself. It celebrates with painful candor the skill, stubbornness, and raw political talent necessary to commemorate with dignity the intricate pain and challenge of a national war. The lives lost cannot be restored but their fierce patriotism here finds its respectful and artful chronicler.
—**Lionel Tiger.** Charles Darwin Professor Emeritus of Anthropology, Rutgers University.

Mosaic
Louis Nelson, an American industrial designer quickly became an expert in the meanings and responsibilities of monuments after winning the once in a lifetime commission to design the mural for the Korean War Veterans Memorial. He was humbled by the prestigious and revered occupants of the sites adjacent to the one where his design would be built on the National Mall: Washington, Lincoln, and Vietnam.

The mission of the memorial was to help American and Korean War vets remember their experiences in Korea, remind all of us of the enormity of lives needlessly lost, and to help them, their families and friends, to heal. Louis tells us some of the fascinating historical information he uncovered, and the vets' stories he was told while researching and designing the memorial. The information and stories all took on new meanings for him, a Cold War Vet, as it did for me, and as it will for you.

—RitaSue Siegel
Strategic Design Consultant

A great story of how a helicopter pilot, a designer, and the Korean War came together to create a monument in Washington.

—**Tucker Viemeister,**
Industrial Designer

"Nelson's Korean War Memorial—a national mantelpiece of portraits—broke the silence of a never-resolved cease-fire, forgotten war.

Mosaic invites us to connect threads Nelson remembers throughout his lifetime, "fixing into the grout" with others the search for what is right and the ability to change the future.

As a grateful veteran and scholarship design student, his long career has impacted our lives regarding food choices, transportation and entertainment, to name a few.

In this memoir, Nelson shows us that to remember is to be put back together, healed and restored for our next chapters. Then we build our best memorial of all—peace."

—The Very Reverend Dr. James A. Kowalski,
Dean Emeritus. The Cathedral of Saint John the Divine

"Mosaic", the story of Louis Nelson's design of the Korean Veteran's Memorial on the Mall in Washington DC, is enlightening, riveting and powerful. The book reveals the fabric of hidden mysteries about a war in which 2.5 million people including 37,000 American men and women, soldiers, sailors and marines died, as well as the seven decades since the never formalized cease-fire, in which nearly 4,000,000 American troops have served. Nelson's life story—as designer, lover, husband (mine)—officer, helicopter pilot and gentleman in the US Army, tells us a full blooded story, one that resounds with artistry and devotion to bringing the story of Korea and the Forgotten War into sharp detail. There are more mysteries here and as he reveals them, it is clear that Louis Nelson, as the designer of the Memorial, is also a writer of insight and ability. After reading it I know more, feel more and understand more about that far off place of history, conflict and the spirit of survival. Thank YOU MISTER NELSON FOR A FINE BOOK.

—Judy Collins.
Author, Singer, Songwriter

Three Soldiers and the Mural

MOSAIC
WAR MONUMENT MYSTERY

For Doug and all these years

LOUIS NELSON

239 PRODUCTIONS
NEW YORK

Copyright © 2021 by Louis Nelson

All rights reserved, including the right to reproduce this book or
portions thereof in any form whatsoever. For information, contact
239 Productions Subsidiary Rights Department,
Post Office Box 995, New York 10025

Published in the United States by 239 Productions
Post Office Box 995 New York 10025

239 is a trademark of 239 Productions.

Book design by Margery Cantor
Cover design by Margery Cantor and Adam Hitt

Text set in Kepler

Photos by Toby Old, Louis Nelson, Elizabeth Freund and Others
Photos by Toby Old copyright ©2020 by Toby Old
Photos by Louis Nelson copyright ©2020 by Louis Nelson
Photos by Elizabeth Freund copyright ©2020 by Elizabeth Freund

Printed and distributed by BookBaby

Library of Congress Control Number has been applied for.

Library of Congress Cataloging-in-Publication Data
Name: Nelson, Louis, 1936- author.
Title: Mosaic. War Monument Mystery/ Louis Nelson
Description: 1. Korea. 2. Wars. 3. Monuments and Memorials. 4. History.
5. Memoir 6. Design and Designers 7. Murals and Muralist
8. Photos and Photographer

ISBN 978-1-09836-609-4 (hardcover)
ISBN 978-1-09836-612-4 (softcover)
ISBN 978-1-09836-613-1 (ebook)

The author has made every attempt to be as accurate as possible
in dates and in the description of historical events.

www.louisnelson.com

The scanning, uploading and distribution of this book via the Internet or via any other means
without the permission of the publisher is illegal and punishable by law. Please purchase only
authorized electronic editions and do not participate in or encourage electronic piracy of
copyrighted materials. Your support of the author's right is appreciated.

Manufactured in the United States of America

First Edition

FOR JUDY, ALWAYS.

*Dedicated to all veterans of all wars,
domestic and foreign, hot and cold.*

*Remembrance is the only Paradise
out of which we cannot be driven.*
—Johann Paul Friedrich Richter,
Geist oder Chrestomathie

CONTENTS

Prelude   A Seminal War   1
One   The Korean War Veterans Memorial   7
Two   Making Things Matter   21
Three   Faces in the Mural   51
Four   Remember   65
Five   General Washington and The Dinner   85
Six   The Struggle for the Lincoln Memorial   99
Seven   The Rift in the Vietnam Memorial   113
Eight   Crisis   121
Nine   A Just War?   131
Ten   Dedication   145
Coda   Mosaic   157

Supplement   169
     Veteran's Day. Michael Veitch. Lyrics.   171
     Acknowledgements. Thank You   173
     Resources. Bibliography   177
     Walls Arise. Poem. Louis Nelson   181
     WALLS. Words by Judy Collins and Louis Nelson.   183
     Remembering the 'Forgotten War'
     Washington Post Op-Ed. July 1995   185
     Designers of National Memorials &
     Monuments on the National Mall (partial list)   187
     Glossary of Acronyms and Abbreviations   189
     Citation for Medal of Honor. Raymond G. Davis   191
     The Author. Louis Nelson   195

PHOTOGRAPHS

Facing Title	MOSAIC xii
	Three Soldiers and the Mural, Louis Nelson xii
Prelude	A Seminal War 1
	Snow and the Korean War Veterans Memorial,
	Elizabeth Freund xxvi
One	The Korean War Veterans Memorial 7
	The Soldiers and the Mural, Louis Nelson 6
Two	Making Things Matter 21
	Child Saluting. WWII Memorial, Toby Old 20
Three	Faces in the Mural 51
	Faces in the Mural, Louis Nelson 50
	The Faces in the Korean War Veterans Memorial Mural,
	double page spread, Louis Nelson 60–61
Four	Remember 65
	Burghers of Calais, Toby Old 64
Five	General Washington and The Dinner 85
	The Medal of Honor &
	The Washington Monument, Toby Old 84
Six	The Struggle for the Lincoln Memorial 99
	Abraham Lincoln (Profile,) Toby Old 98
Seven	The Rift in the Vietnam Memorial 113
	Three Soldiers., Toby Old 112
Eight	Crisis 121
	Korean Mural and Soldiers, Louis Nelson 120
Nine	A Just War? 131
	Tomb of the Unknown Soldier, Toby Old 130

Ten	Dedication 145
	President Clinton, General Ivany, the Mural, and a Soldier, U.S. Government Photograph 144
	The Mural at the Korean War Veterans Memorial, East Section, Louis Nelson 153
	Double page spread, Louis Nelson 154–155
Coda	Mosaic 157
	Faces of Some of the Missing 9/11 New York, Toby Old 156
Supplement	*The Reflecting Pool at Twilight,* Toby Old 168

MOSAIC

Snow and the Korean War Veterans Memorial

This is to all who find themselves
Not playing on the old school yard

PRELUDE
A SEMINAL WAR

The sky was blue on that September day in 1950, as it was on the following day. The third day it rained. Newly arrived in South Korea, his airborne company was composed of highly motivated trained veterans. Company Commander Bill Weber fought battles in the South Pacific and Okinawa during WWII. His men were cocky and believed they would annihilate the North Koreans with little effort. Within days, his unit was ambushed; he lost his radio operator, taking a bullet in the head. Instantly he and his troops could see that the North Korean troops were very well trained, disciplined and a strong adversary. And in short order other units at the Chosin Reservoir will also learn the Red Chinese are similarly trained.

Weeks later, Weber was on his walkie-talkie when a grenade exploded; he dropped the phone, went to pick it up only to realize his right arm was gone.

The air of this Washington July is humid and presses on me. The sun beats down on the steps of the Lincoln Memorial. Ahead, the cooling water of the Reflecting Pool, the blue sky and the Washington Monument brilliantly reflected on its calm surface, appearing in a long mirror. To my left, a green lawn, trees and the black granite wall of names on the Vietnam Veterans Memorial. To my right I see the glistening stainless-steel statues of the Korean War soldiers passing a long gray granite wall of faces, portraits of the men and women supporting them... The Korean War Veterans Memorial. Visitors are around me, speaking in hushed tones. Independence Day on the National Mall. Events of the long past start to take on new meanings for me.

Sixty years ago, North Korea invaded South Korea. Korea became America's first war engaged with the new United Nations, an historic event as our country enjoyed peace-time growth after the Second World War, supporting an enriched standard of living as strategic changes vibrated in the Soviet Union. Korea was the first war the United States fought against the Chinese Communists. And, it is the first war in the past century we didn't win.

We've not won a war since 1945.*

⸙

In 1990, I was asked to design the mural at the Korean Veterans Memorial on the Mall in Washington, DC. Beginning the design, I read countless books on the history of the war, the battles that took place. I walked the Mall, visited my neighbors, Lincoln, Vietnam and Washington. I studied archival photographs. Living with faces of those who served, I began to see a power in their gazes, a story told in their eyes, the freezing weather, their indispensable self-confidence, determination and love.

Our need to remember hooks us to the core of what happened in those days in Korea, to the essence of the men and women, and prompts questions as to "why" and "how." As we remember, we are linked together, each bringing our own sense of the grimness of the war—perhaps in the shooting and fighting of the battles, or at home, supporting or worrying about our loved ones. Collectively, we better understand this specialness—and how that moment long ago has skipped to this day, vibrating with unanticipated consequences in a new world of technological threats, challenging an unsettling peace. In the end, responding to these challenges enables us to move forward to the next stage in our lives.

---

*The 1991 Gulf War ended with a ceasefire after 100 hours of intense and devastating combat. Kuwait was liberated. General Schwarzkopf did not carry the war to Baghdad's surrender, nor disarm the Iraq army because of concerns of fracturing the coalition. Iraq forces retained their arms to be used another day. And, they were used another day against the Kurds. Further, this 1991 Gulf War would, with the erroneous discovery of "weapons of mass destruction" eventually erupt into the 2003 Iraq War, ending with the capture of Saddam Hussein and years of ongoing insurgency, sectarian violence and internal unrest if not war.

Early during World War II, there were honor rolls of names in each of the town squares in many of America's cities. In my Astoria, Queens, New York neighborhood square, a list of names was carefully lettered on a white-painted wall taking up most of this small triangle of green park on Northern Boulevard, just a few blocks away from my apartment. Some of the names had gold stars. I didn't know any of them. I was seven years old then, 1944. D-Day was about to happen. I remember a family dressed in their Sunday finest, going to church. Perhaps then to a cemetery, probably Calvary, a long way from where I lived. A long way from home. I could tell something unusual was happening. My friend told me that his parents had attended a service and paid their respects to the mother; her son had been a soldier. I don't recall him saying a memorial service and a "viewing." Thinking back, I realize that most of the Americans who were killed were probably buried in a military cemetery in Europe. A war was going on. A different war. It was another time.

Although the Korean War was rarely discussed, seldom mentioned... forgotten by nearly everyone... North Korea was slowly reemerging—becoming increasingly strategic, affecting global relations in politics, economics and technology, underpinned with threatening hostility, maintaining a struggling economy and poorly fed citizens—all the while South Korea was prospering. The region, with China and Japan, had become a focus of growing uncertainty. It has become apparent how important the Korean War was in our lives, its proper place in the sequence of this nation's conflicts—from the Civil War to the War on Terror—and its place in our future. In this post-World War II period of extraordinary growth in jobs and peace, Korea was the first war of confusion after the long hard-won victories of the terrible *War to End All Wars* and *The Good War*, World War I and World War II respectively. Korea was the start of a long, complicated sequence of wars we did not clearly win as we became engaged in more complex relations, new global alliances and bitter contests with Communism.

We have chosen to build memorials for those wars we won, and to those who served. The Cold War was passed over with a sense of unease; the current wars in Iraq and Afghanistan, and now Syria, seems to come back at us in an unending cycle of failed strategies. If there was a lesson to be learned from the memorials and monuments we built, we seem to have forgotten it; our leaders had become trapped in their own affairs, unable to remember the war lessons honored on the National Mall and rarely, it seems, to reach across the aisle to solve the military and humane issues for the American public . . . and move out of an unending war mode.

Much of the cycle of war and redemption is written into the ancient tale of Cain and Abel. Cain and God had worked out a deal, as the ancient scribes have written. They negotiated a settlement so that Cain could live with his mark. Today, are we seeing two new brothers, one in the North and the other in the South . . . plus a cousin in America, acting out the old story of resentment and threats leading to a new kind of deal? Has the "flood" been replaced by a nuclear threat, while others sit paralyzed with uncertainty?

The Korean War Veterans Memorial commemorates those men and women who fought, illuminating through its figurative design of face and form the individuals who served and silently came home. By act of Congress in 1986, the Korean War Veterans Memorial was the first memorial dedicated to the service of the men and women in battle—instead of a president, or a list of those who died.

Oscillating threats from North Korea have intensified in 2017 under its new leader Kim Jong-un as he flexes his nation's muscle, pulling us back into the Cold War era of uncertainty and increased regional unrest for the people and the governments of Japan and South Korea. China seems to stand stoic as America's President Trump parries to counter the threat. The uncertainty endures. In these pages is the story of how I have come to believe the Korean War is the seminal war of the last century, pressing into our lives today. Here are the stories of men and women, surrounding the commemoration of a great and nearly forgotten war of America. And here is the story of how the Korean War Veterans Memorial speaks to its neighbors, the Vietnam Veterans Memorial and the Lincoln Memorial, stories of those who made decisions about the battles, battles across the trenches and battles across the aisle. Stories from a stranger, a man-on-a-horse—monuments to your neighbor. Heroes and Devils.

Seemingly a local war, America soon became aware we were in a hot war with Communism. The Korean War extended into regional tensions within China, the Soviet Union and the United Nations, and back to WWII's unsolved cultural boundaries—echoing farther back to the earliest of the Crusades. There is something about our human nature pressing to settle disparities by battle.

A new modern era starts in 1953 with the Korean War's ceasefire, more than sixty years ago—a Hot War sliding into a Cold War and an Iron Curtain already dropped in Europe between the East and the West. Soon America, while facing a challenge in a space race, will evolve in a period of shivering international politics; a country with an expanding economy in full recovery from the Good War, enriching its citizens living conditions while escalating development of nuclear power and an ever-present threat of an atomic holocaust. That fear may be the enduring monument to this Cold War. Today, after decades of complex dramas and global economic success, we seem not to be able to support our standard of living as too many citizens struggle to even gain a foothold, while a few others gather the wealth that was promised to hard workers in this American way of life . . . a peace that is not a peace we can afford.

Here, on these pages is the enduring meaning of the "forgotten war"; about how that war affected its veterans, which led to its memorial and the mural; and the process of designing the mural. My hope is that you will come away with a greater understanding of the curious importance of the Korean War as a fulcrum in our line of wars rendering a sense of need to find another way of making decisions to resolve conflict.

Today, the last war we clearly won was World War II in 1945. The last memorials we built was for World War II in 2004 and Martin Luther King Jr in 2011, one commemorating a distant "good war," the other honoring one who faced a war within ourselves. With all the challenges and wars we faced, and the battles for equal rights, it has been a chaotic path—fraught with the drama of the democratic process, not always pretty, as democracy is not always sweet. But oh, so beautiful, so full of mystery, human error and travail.

The Soldiers and the Mural

Running for their lives
And not much else

ONE
THE KOREAN WAR VETERANS MEMORIAL

Bill Lascheid, a newly commissioned Navy surgeon was in a jeep heading to the "Punchbowl" in the eastern section of the combat line, fighting off the dust and haze while enamored by the terrain and the drama of the Korean mountains. He was fresh from training at Marine Camp Lejeune and combat fit. Bill had a smile on his lips and determination in his eyes. Two days later, with shells exploding around him, he jumped into a bunker for cover. A neighboring bunker was hit. Bill crawled over to administer aid to a fallen Marine; he got him onto a stretcher, and finally to a helicopter and a quick take off. Day 1 and 2 in Korea for Bill Lascheid.

Forty years and three months after the invasion of South Korea, they called. It was an early Autumn morning in 1990. Bill Lecky, a Washington, DC, architect was on the phone. It seemed I had been waiting for this call my whole life.

I first met William P. Lecky the year before when I served on the Design Arts Grants Committee of the National Endowment for the Arts. In one of the last sessions, early in the 1989-1990 season, Bill and I became friendly. A gentle soft-spoken man, he had a knowing look in his eyes and a ready smile. Now Bill was calling to say that he was on the team to design the new Korean War Veterans Memorial and was seeking some information. (I knew he and his partner Kent Cooper, were the Architects-of-Record for the Vietnam Veterans Memorial). He said he was calling to see if I could recommend a graphic designer to create the mural for this new memorial. I said, "Of course" and started to mention a couple names, then blurted out my own. "ME!" Bill chuckled and said he had expected I'd say that. He asked if I could come to Washington in a couple of weeks and meet with the Advisory Board to discuss my experience and approach to this assignment. He explained the board was led by General Richard Stilwell and mentioned the names of other board members. They would be interviewing four designers. Later I learned that two of them were my friends: Michael Donovan of Donovan/Green and Lou Dorfsman, the noted head of design for CBS. Michael, however, told me over lunch years subsequently that when he had heard I was also a candidate, he dropped out. The third candidate was a leading poster designer for the movie industry in Los Angeles.

I blocked out a number of different directions to discuss with the Board. Finally, I decided to tell the group how this war affected my life and the decisions I made as I entered college and my design education, and the subsequent steps of my life—being in ROTC, the Army, learning to fly a helicopter, sent to West Germany when a wall was built in Berlin, effects of the Cuban Missile Crisis, returning to civilian life, graduate school and some of the highlights of my design career, all leading to meeting Bill Lecky at the National Endowment for the Arts. Preferring to put things down on paper, I drafted a list of related issues regarding Korea: the service of those who served, who they were and what they did, the key sites during this three-year war, the priorities of Americans to build a life in the new found prosperity after the success of WWII. I flew to Washington, DC on a glistening sunny day. Entering Bill's Georgetown architectural office, I was welcomed by his partner, Kent Cooper, a tall, big fellow with a genuine smile and an outstretched hand, saying how glad he was to meet me. I immediately liked him. I met each of the twelve board members present: among them, there were General Richard Stilwell, serious yet cordial; General Raymond Davis, pleasant with gentle eyes; and Col.* Rosemary McCarthy, very cheerful, who said her job was to make sure women were represented in this memorial. I gave my talk, showed a few slides of my projects, answered some questions, said, "thank you and it would be a privilege to work with you," and left. The Board had seemed quite

---

*The author decided to use *The Chicago Manual of Style* terminology for military abbreviations of rank throughout the book as different abbreviations are used by the U.S. Army, the Marine Corp and the U.S. Air Force.

receptive; I thought I did a good job. At least I was feeling pretty positive as I flew back to New York... and hopeful. A few weeks later, on a bright afternoon with light streaming thru the windows of my Greenwich Village office, sitting with Elliot Goldman, a client and dear friend discussing his brand and identity, Bill Lecky called again.

He said they selected me. "The location of the memorial will be just to the right of the Lincoln Memorial—as you're looking towards the Washington Monument from Lincoln's feet. At Lincoln's left hand is the successful Vietnam Memorial. At his right will be the Korean War Veterans Memorial." Hung up the phone and I think I screamed, "We got it." I was filled with excitement and pride. And anxiety. I can't minimize this. I immediately thought, *This is going to be standing for a while. How do I deal with designing a mural with such prestigious and revered neighbors?*

In my first weeks of planning the Korean War Veterans Memorial Mural, I added to the list I had made, outlining the chronology of the events to help me remember and better understand what happened before the war and as a result of the war: the politics, the rivalry between Truman and MacArthur, and the stories of Heartbreak Ridge, Pork Chop Hill and Chosin Reservoir. I filled myself with all I could read about the Korean War.

Korea was different. Different, because most Americans forgot this war; different, because Korea was the first war abated in a ceasefire; because it was the first war we fought with the United Nations; and because it was the first war we fought the Chinese Communists, face to face; and, as mentioned, different because it was the first significant war in the modern era we did not clearly win.

Looking back from 1990, this war provided a mid-century focal point—easily ignored because it was so remote. Stalin had died near the end of the war in 1953 and his legacy slipped in the face of Khrushchev's power and personality; by 1957 Sputnik was beeping overhead, distracting America with the burgeoning space race, with the Soviet Union ahead of us. And even as our country was enjoying a rising standard of living, the ever-present knowledge that the Soviets had nuclear capabilities left us with a feeling of uncertainty.

From 1910 and for the next thirty-five years, Japan ruled Korea as its colony. After she lost the Second World War, the leaders of the Allies (Churchill, Roosevelt, and Chiang Kai-shek, with Stalin attending) decided Japan relinquish all her colonies, including Korea. Thus, Japan's colonial rule of its neighbor ended at the Potsdam Conference in 1945. A subsequent conference in Moscow decided to divide Korea into north and south sectors. Korea was placed under a Four-power administered "Trusteeship" with a stipulation that it hold free elections. Soon, failure to hold the mandated democratic elections prompted U.S. administrators and Communist leaders to agree and divide Korea at the 38th parallel: to the north, the Democratic People's Republic of Korea (DPRK), influenced by China and the Soviet Union; and to the south, the Republic of Korea (ROK), supported by the West, the United Nations and the United States.

After a span of five short years, on Sunday, June 25th, 1950, North Korea crossed the 38th Parallel and invaded South Korea in their quest to unify Korea, pushing southward and signaling a Communist threat to Japan and other countries in the Far East. President Truman on receiving word late on Saturday night, June 24th when on a weekend family visit in Independence, Missouri, returned to Washington DC on Sunday, consulted with his Secretary of State, Dean Acheson, his Secretary of Defense, Louis Johnson, and his Chairman of the Joint Chiefs General Omar Bradley and other officials. He most certainly was not pleased by this action of North Korea. Perhaps surprised, as he knew in detail the abiding international agreements. On that Sunday morning, Truman stood at the threshold of the Cold War, the Nuclear Era and the modern second half of the 20th Century. At his back he had ended World War II when he decided to use the atomic bomb to shorten the war. In these brief few years, he had initiated the Truman Doctrine and was largely responsible for nurturing the Marshall Plan to rebuild a Europe devastated by the war. Along the way, he integrated the segregated American Armed Forces.

On the following Monday morning, Truman spoke at length with Dean Acheson. In the ensuing three days, he consulted further with his military and civilian advisors, chiefs of the Air Force and Navy (General Hoyt Vandenberg and Admiral Forrest Sherman), Army Chief of Staff, General J. Lawton Collins, Dean Rusk, (Assistant Secretary of State for East Asian and Pacific Affairs) and leaders of Congress. With deep thought and without much ado, President Harry S. Truman ordered American troops into South Korea, calling the order a "Police Action," and petitioned the United Nations to intervene. The UN Security Council approved the use of force and added United Nations troops to restore order. Truman's action was the first time America entered a war without Congressional authorization. It would set the tone for political-military maneuvers for the coming decades. Vietnam would follow under President Johnson's direction.*

General Douglas MacArthur, commanding US Forces in the Far East in 1950 was put in command of the UN Forces in Korea. He ordered Task Force Smith—a regimental combat team of 406 infantry soldiers led by Lt. Col. Charles B. Smith—to land in Pusan on the southeast coast of Korea. They established a perimeter at Taejon and on July 5, 1950, moved on to Osan, south of Seoul, to hold against the enemy. But the US Army of 1950 was not the 1945 winning army of WWII. Task Force Smith was composed of mostly untrained American teenagers, poorly equipped, under-armed and lacking adequate ammunition. The force met a superior North Korean tank column and engaged in the Battle of Osan. North Korea then added another column of tanks. The soldiers of Task Force Smith held as best as they could, eventually withdrawing, which turned into a rout. They were badly defeated and pulled back to the Pusan perimeter.

In the meantime, MacArthur conceived a new plan. A couple months later, on September 15, 1950 with all units in place, he initiated an "end run." In secret, a massive amphibious force landed at Inchon, behind enemy lines on the west coast, freeing Seoul from the North Korean grip. MacArthur had placed Major General Edward "Ned" Almond in charge of X Corps, a force composed of American and United Nations elements. Attached to X Corps was the 1st Marine Division, commanded by Major General Oliver Prince Smith. Almond's plan was to deploy his forces north toward Chosin Reservoir, using ships to move the 1st Marine Division around the Korean peninsula and up the coast to Wonsan. Concurrently, General Walton Walker's Eighth Army will turn north toward the Yalu River. At the beginning of October 1950, UN Forces pushed north past the 38th parallel. While that was happening, Smith brought his Marine division back to Inchon, loaded onto ships, steamed

---

*History fully understands that military advisors were first sent to Vietnam by President Eisenhower, with more troops added by President Kennedy, dramatically increased by President Johnson, slowly reduced by President Nixon and ended by President Ford.

around the southern peninsular, headed north and arrived at Wonsan. After the harbor was freed of mines, Smith debarked and moved his twenty thousand men past Hagaru deep into North Korea. His objective was Chosin Reservoir. Moving into the mountains, he established units in and around Yudam-ni and Hill 1282. The strategic Toktong Pass was in the neighborhood. This was high country and cold beyond belief. Snow was falling. The units dug-in as best they could in frozen ground. They established positions and fields-of-fire to defend their perimeter and the hill. On the night of October 19th, the Marines were surprised by Communist Chinese who earlier had come down from the north to aid the North Koreans. Hundreds of thousands. Hidden and invisible during the day, the Chinese were lying in wait for the Marines to arrive. It was reported that General MacArthur, suspicious of Chinese movement into the area, on a return flight to Japan personally made a daytime aerial surveillance of the area to verify evidence of any Chinese presence. He found none. Hampton Sides quotes historian S.L.A. Marshall as saying the Red Chinese forces was a "phantom which casts no shadow. Its main secrets—its strength, its position, and its initiative—had been kept to perfection, and therefore it was doubly armed." Here and in many other positions in the mountains, the Chinese fought the Marines that night and many subsequent nights, always in the pitch-black of darkness—first blasting horns and banging pots and pans, creating a racket to disorient the Americans. Then, in ominous silence, they regrouped and waited. Instantly, without warning, the Red Chinese attacked the Marines in vicious numbers, firing their rifles while greatly out numbering the Americans. Night after night. Reports of vast numbers of Chinese Communist units in North Korea were sent to Almond and MacArthur. They were ignored—Army intelligence not supporting what the troops were experiencing. Piles of dead Chinese bodies grew by the hundreds and more. Examination showed they were ill prepared, some without weapons, expected to pick up guns as comrades fell. They lacked overcoats. Few had gloves. Poor shoes. To rest, they were expected to pair off with another and sleep entwined.

The Marines lost vast numbers of soldiers as well. So much that Smith decided to move back. Historically, he said, "Retreat, hell! We're not retreating, we're advancing in a different direction." It was also called a "breakout." With Almond's and MacArthur's approval, units along the long single road leading into the mountains and Chosin Reservoir started to regroup. However, Fox Company of the Second Battalion, Seventh Regiment was isolated and nearly decimated, losing 118 casualties in the Company. A special detachment was arranged by Smith to rescue his unit, led by Lieutenant Colonel Raymond Davis with his Marine battalion. (The same Raymond Davis who later will sit on the Korean War Veterans Memorial Advisory Board). Marine platoon leader Lieutenant Kurt Chew-Een Lee, selected by Davis, was the "pathfinder" in the lead. Davis with Lee and his battalion moved on foot in the dark, avoiding the roads and paths in radio silence, walking without chatter for ten or more miles up and down mountains and valley. Supported only with ancient outdated Japanese maps, a compass and good Marine instinct, Fox Company was found. Before the break of dawn, the remaining soldiers of the distressed company were rescued. With no time to rest, Davis and his battalion, along with Fox Company now prepared to join the long withdrawal on the narrow single road back toward Wonsan, with heavy fighting by the Red Chinese, mile after mile along the route.

The Battle of Chosin was deadly. By the time 22,215 Marines evacuated Wonsan by ship, 30,000 Chinese were killed, and thousands wounded; 750 Marines were killed and 3,000 wounded.* These statistics added to others in other battles would grow significantly during the full 36 months of the war.

At the end of eight months of hostile and deadly battles, in February 1951, peace talks were informally initiated. On July 10th they were formally started in Kaesong and proceeded slowly with gaps between meetings. In another few months, on October 25, 1951, meetings formally commenced between the UN Forces and North Korea in Panmunjom located within the Demilitarized Zone. The discussion centered on the repatriation of prisoners-of-war, a fixed demilitarized zone and the realization of a ceasefire. After three years of bloody and exhausting conflict, the United Nations representatives were able to enforce a resolution coming out of the truce talks at Panmunjom. Ceasefire was pro-

---

* Data and statistics for America's wars are available from the Department of Defense, Department of the Army, Department of the Navy and various veterans' groups. In many instances, the term "casualties" can include injured, wounded, dead (battle and non-battle) and captured. Because of differences in the organizational structure of the statistics, it has been difficult to correlate and validate data for a specific reference. The author has made every attempt to be as accurate as possible.

claimed on July 27, 1953—only to be put to the test through six long decades of continuous taunts and skirmishes; arriving, as the world today witnesses, a new round in the continuing drama between North and South Korea complicated with the threat from the North of nuclear missile attacks.

Few of us in the States remember the details. However, neither the United States nor the Soviet Union, nor Communist China, nor the United Nations were signatory to the "ceasefire." A peace treaty or surrender was never accomplished. What may surprise many is that the North and the South did not sign the "ceasefire" either. The North, Democratic People's Republic of Korea (DPRK) had refused to return to the table to complete the agreement; and the South, Republic of Korea (ROK) simply stood fast—not taking any overt action against the North. The ceasefire agreement ended resulting in no more than a verbal formality, threatening the coming decades.

When I started to envision the mural and evolve a concept, I talked with a number of veterans. The one thing I heard over and over is their hope for a memorial that would recreate their defining moment of service in "their" war. They spoke about their jobs and the battles and the weather, some spoke of what they did and the tanks and planes and their friends.

Bill Weber, a thin lanky 1st Lieutenant commanding an airborne infantry company, had landed at an airfield just south of Seoul to reinforce the invading amphibious troops who pressed on from Incheon into Seoul. The sky was blue on that September day, as on the following day. His men believed they would annihilate the North Koreans with little effort. Within days, his column was ambushed by the North. He lost his radio operator, taking a bullet in the head. Instantly he and his troops could see that the North Korean troops, and in short order, the Red Chinese were very well trained, disciplined and a strong adversary. Some sixty-seven years had passed when he related his story to me with absolute clarity, in an un-halting voice as if it had happened just the day before. Still tall and lanky, now a retired Colonel, his face showing the lines of every battle, Bill shook his head, saying he remembered witnessing China's disregard for human life, its troops massed in numerical superiority over the Americans, engaged in countless attacks against a hill top position or a road we Americans thought impossible for them to win. He also recalled fighting in sub-zero temperatures, where their urine would freeze in seconds as they relieved themselves. The Chinese outnumbered them 15:1.

In his fifth month in Korea, Bill was talking on a walkie-talkie when a grenade exploded; he dropped the phone, went to pick it up only to realize his right arm was gone. He continued to lead his company and within an hour or two, his left leg too had been severed in a blast from another grenade. As he's telling me this, I couldn't believe the Chinese had been able to get so close as to toss the grenades. Nor could I believe this man had not stopped but instead, kept going, engaging the enemy. This was decades before the RPG (rocket-propelled grenades) used in Iraq and Afghanistan. Luckily, Bill was treated in his Battalion aid station. Lucky, because he was in shock, in and out of consciousness and near death, but had grown to know those doctors in the months prior. When one of them recognized Bill lying on a stretcher, the doctor immediately gave him what was needed to stabilize the trauma and had him evacuated by helicopter to a Swedish Army Hospital in South Korea, then to Japan and on to Hawaii and the States for recovery and rehabilitation. In route, ever responsible, Bill asked after his unit and learned that he had lost thirty-eight men—about 30% of his company.

South Korean and US troops had forged to the Yalu River, which forms the border between North Korea and China. This successful onslaught resulted in China entering the war in the mountains near Chosin Reservoir, pushing UN Forces back with great losses in the bitter freezing cold of the Korean winter. When Smith's First Marine Division evacuated Wonsan, Seoul was again evacuated and occupied by the North, but soon regained by the South. MacArthur began threatening to destroy China by pressing northward once more; the General wished to cross the Yalu River into China and announced he was considering using atomic weapons, all without Truman's knowledge or approval—and all contrary to the decisions made at an earlier meeting on Wake Island, between the President and himself. Truman was livid. There were recriminations and fireworks in the press, and I imagine lots said privately. In April 1951, Truman relieved MacArthur of his command, replacing him with General Matthew B. Ridgway. Within a matter of months, on July 10th the peace talks commenced, were delayed and restarted in October at Panmunjom between the UN Forces and North Korea. Coupled with this, it was an election year. Truman lost. In January 1953, Dwight D. Eisenhower, the hero of World War II, became the 34th President of the United States.

From June 1951 to July 1953, the Korean War entered a period of peace talks in Panmunjom, but the battles raged on. After attending to the Marine's wounds in the bunker and getting him safely to a helicopter, Bill Lascheid continued with his work at the E Medical Unit. Under heavy fighting and historic efforts, the unit was able to evacuate one thousand soldiers with helicopters that carried only five soldiers at a time. He frequently administered to local women and children at the sick bay. South Korean civilians being caught in the middle of a war needed medical help from the harm they endured. More heavy fighting and "still no progress with the peace talks," Lascheid wrote in letters home. "Extraordinary results performed on an amazing degree of injury and damage to a Marine's body" and "frequently multiple injuries . . . treated by the miraculous skill of the medical staff." Fire and burns, "there's nothing like the odor of burnt skin . . ." For Christmas 1951, they cut down a tree, made ornament balls from the silver foil of cigarette packages and red streamers from surgical gauze tinted with mercurochrome. Finally, they hung the silver balls on the tree, and wrapped it with the red streamers. They gathered around and sang Christmas carols while shells exploded in the distance. Frequently they had to perform surgery with minimal lighting. When the fighting became more intense, numbingly loud and the power went out, the surgical team would take flashlights, shine them on the wound and the operation would continue; and when the shelling would worsen, the lead surgeon would burst into song, "You are my sunshine, my only sunshine, you make me happy when skies are grey. . . ." The others around the table would harmonize. Once a departing surgeon gave Bill a ukulele. He learned to play it. He also played bridge but stayed away from poker. The ukulele came home with him and was handed down to his son who also learned to play, and then to his son's son.

In the spring of 1953, while Lascheid continued his surgical service, John Phillips arrived by ship in Pusan, Korea directly from Army Basic Training in the States. An enlisted man in the 31st Regiment, 7th Infantry Division, John was assigned as a heavy machine gun operator in a heavy weapons company, based ten miles in the western section of what will be called the DMZ. He was nervous about what was facing him. He saw civilians begging for help and children with outstretched hands for candy. Ominously, he was assigned to an isolated outpost designated "West View," west of the famous Pork Chop

Hill and south of Old Baldy. Things were reasonably stable at that time, not much troop movement, whereas earlier—1950–1951—the entire area was dominated with troop movements and some military disasters, including the Battle of Chosin Reservoir in the north. The "action" at John's location, the 2nd Pork Chop Hill, was at night during July 1953. As John related, the North Koreans and Chinese would rush by, banging pots and pans and whatever else to make a racket to distract and create the greatest amount of fear in the pitch-black night; then they would return to their earlier positions, only to come back in a second wave, now shooting to take the objective, this hilltop or another. Nothing made sense or seemed logical, but this was a new war with a new culture. In the dark, John couldn't see much in this remote location; he was cut off from everyone and told not to fire indiscriminately because it would disclose his position. It was lonely there; yet, during the day, the living standard was "pretty good"—he was able to have "hot meals five times a week. Hot breakfast with pancakes, bacon, coffee. Two beers per person a day." The spring weather was hot and humid—somewhat like Washington, DC, in August. There were thunderstorms and heavy downpours—three to four inches of water in the trenches. Wet feet and jock itch were prevalent. The North, meanwhile, would play Glenn Miller music on loudspeakers, then taunt the Americans about what their girlfriends were doing with their best friends back in the States. American tastes, however, had moved on. Patti Page, Jo Stafford, Nat King Cole and Perry Como were topping the charts back in the States, with songs such as "Tennessee Waltz," "Doggie in the Window," "Mona Lisa," "You Belong to Me," "How High the Moon." "Come On-a My House," and "Cold, Cold Heart" were among the top with Tony Bennett and Rosemary Clooney. And the Weavers with "Goodnight Irene." John missed hearing these tunes. The stress was enormous; the only relief came from the jokes his buddies liked to play. As it turned out, the jokes were about the food or the showers. When pressed, John said it was mostly teasing each other about what their girlfriends were doing back home. Heckling! Of course, it could turn nasty. He didn't want to say more than that.

His unit was on a rotating schedule with a fresh group taking his place. Within two days there was a major push by the North and everyone in the new unit was killed. Everybody! Later, when John "rotated" back, he saw them one last time: "Fifty bodies stacked along the roadside awaiting removal." He said there was no need for a parade when he got home . . . he and his unit had done their job and now he needed to get back to work.

It was in listening to these three veterans as well as to myriad others that I began to understand what the vets were looking for in the memorial: help in remembering what they did in Korea and what had been lost . . . and who. More Americans have served in this war for freedom than you would think—6.8 million. 36,500 were killed in the 3 years during this war on the Korean peninsula; 33,739 of them in combat. In addition, American forces were reinforced with troops from the Korean Service Corps (KATUSA). These forces, a total of 43,600 South Korean individuals were "embedded" with American forces. They experienced a casualty rate of over 27%, 8,127 killed in action. This brings the total American forces (reinforced by KATUSA) killed to 41,866 in three years of combat. The magnitude of loss in such a short time is startling when you consider that in the ten to twenty-year Vietnam War the total number of those killed was 58,220. I was suddenly aware that this memorial was likely to affect tens of thousands of visitors from all fifty of the United States and from untold allied countries of the World—those who had lost relatives and friends in the US military, as well as those who mourn the losses of lives in both North and South Korea

Years later, Bill Lascheid, the now battle experienced Navy surgeon, back in the United States, and in his own medical practice writes—

1977. I had a practice in Pittsburg(h), Pennsylvania . . . arrived home late one winter night just as the telephone was ringing. My wife picked up the phone, and the caller asked if this was the home of Dr. Lascheid. She replied that it was, assuming it was a patient . . . handed the phone to me as I walked in the door. The caller identified himself as a Marine who had been wounded in Korea.

"Did you serve in Korea?" the caller asked. I said I had. He asked whether I'd served with the 1st Battalion, 1st Marine Division and I replied, "I had."

He then identified himself as the Marine who had been wounded in that bunker!

In words broken with emotion, the former Marine said that while I was running alongside the gurney tending to his wounds, he tried to focus on the name on my uniform. He was slipping in and out of consciousness, yet he wanted to memorize the name of the young doctor tending to him. He noted that it was an unusual name and spelling—Lascheid.

After he returned home and recovered, he built a career as a salesman and traveled extensively. Through the years, as he went from city to city, he'd pore through phone books, looking for a Dr. Lascheid. He had done the same on his current trip to Pittsburgh.

After telling me his story the caller concluded abruptly.

"Thank you for saving my life" he blurted out. "I've been looking for you all these years to say thank you."

With that, he hung up . . . I didn't get the chance to say anything in return. The Marine's mission was apparently accomplished.

—Bill Lascheid. A private memoir

Child Saluting, WW II Memorial

To the drumming of their own desperate hearts
To the drumming of their own desperate hearts

TWO
MAKING THINGS MATTER

The world was changing. I couldn't have said it then. It was 1950 and I wouldn't have known it. All was quiet, settling down after the war. Seems this was an era of silence, at least in my family, in my neighborhood. Halfway around the world, South Korea was invaded by the North and American troops were in combat over there. In a few years, John Phillips will be manning a heavy-duty machine gun near Old Baldy in Korea, and Pork Chop Hill. In the dark, John couldn't see much; he was cut off from everyone and told not to fire indiscriminately because it would disclose his position. It was lonely there. His unit was on a rotating schedule with a fresh group now taking his place. Within two days there was a major push by the North. Everybody in the new unit was killed. Everybody! I was about to enter high school.

I didn't know anything about Korea then. Perhaps Mom and Dad did.

We did things a certain way in those days, lived with traditions learned from our mothers and grandmothers when we were young. Astoria was a tight-knit community of working-class families, first- and second-generation Irish and Italian Americans with an abiding respect for their Roman Catholic Mass and for America. As for my family, we were the only Norwegians in the neighborhood. Our grandparents lived around the corner, the next street over. My family was Lutheran. Or at least Mom was. My sister and I were raised accordingly. I don't think my grandmother and grandfather, my dad's parents, went to church. Certainly not my father. Yet, they respected people.

Dad was a serious man, a self-taught electrical engineer, spending long hours at work on special "war" electronic products. Before the war, he was an audio engineer, designing and installing custom built hi-fi music systems for high-end residences, including those of Cole Porter, Ethel Merman and other celebrities. He would come home late, tired; needing to bring in extra income to cover expenses. He was gone much of the time; held two jobs after the War, as I remember. Nearly six feet tall and thin, fine hair tending to recede; wore a trimmed mustache. He smiled and laughed more frequently when I was younger, before the War.

Dorothy came in April 1942. I was five and a half. Dad being an avid photographer, there were lots of photos of her, and me holding her. But what I remember most when she was a baby is dad balancing Dorothy standing in the palm of his hand as he held her feet and raised her high above his head, a big proud smile on his lips. Five years was a big difference between us. It seemed Dorothy always had a sense of freedom and ease about her. I was proper and needed to have all my work done and in order. Once, mom was in a rant about something Dorothy did and ran after her shaking a wooden spoon. Unusual for mom, but she looked in a terror. I called out, "You can't do that, Mom." Older and still in school, after having cookies and milk in our stockinged feet, we'd laugh saying we had "foot problems" and played stepping on each other's feet. Older still, at Christmas time we'd watch Alastair Sim's *A Christmas Carol*. To this day, every Christmas we'll call each other to see if we saw the movie. We both were out of college and me out of the service and graduate school, both on our way in our careers; Dorothy would call occasionally, not happy about one thing or another. We'd talk. And talk some more.

So, with Dad working long hours, it was Mom who raised me and my sister. She cooked and scrubbed our clothes on a washboard in the tub of our 3rd floor apartment. I remember going up the stairs, past the 5th floor, the top story, to the roof where Mom would be hanging the laundry to dry in the sun and a New York breeze on clothes lines suspended from black posts. One time she took me to the roof overlooking Astoria's main thoroughfare, Steinway Street, to see President Roosevelt; he was coming from LaGuardia Airport and headed into Manhattan. Somehow Mom knew both the time and route of his motorcade—a series of black cars is all I recall, going pretty fast, only a block away past the Borden's milk building, and in seconds he was gone, onto Northern Boulevard, then Queens Plaza, onto the Queensboro Bridge and into the City. Gone! But we saw him, top down in his limo, I recall.

Every now and then, Dad would help Mom put care packages together for her relatives in Norway. Life was hard in the "Old Country," hard here too. And, with the ongoing war, rationing and blackout conditions at night were accepted as the norm. Sacrifices had to be made. Mom and Dad taught my sister and me about simple ethics, right from wrong and how to treat people and to be polite. My grandfather, a hard-working stoker at the Sunshine Biscuits bakery, and my dad, too, would stop when a hearse passed by and everyone on the street would do the same, watching in silence. Men would tip their hats to women. They taught us the importance of working hard and succeeding. Mom was always positive. Always had a smile. After the war she started painting landscapes in oils. She started with paint-by-the-numbers and moved on to her own compositions. As I grew older, Dad seemed to worry more and more. As best I could figure, his company moved further out on Long Island making his commute longer; costs were increasing, as his salary remained stagnant. I also suppose, not having a college degree, he was paid a lower salary even while holding significant management responsibilities.

My grandmother, "Nana," lived around the corner from us. Years later, I remember Nana had my cousin Andrew's photo on the mantelpiece. His eyes smiled as he looked out at us. The picture was taken just before the Korean War; he was dressed in his uniform. Stationed here in New York, he met my Aunt Jenny, my grandparent's daughter, and in short order wanted to marry her. He never did. He received orders to Japan, and soon left. Andrew was a welder with a combat engineer unit. After serving, he returned to his home in Montana, started working in the East Helena smelter, walking in the steps of his father, Helmer, my mother's brother. Before the war, when we visited my mother's family in Montana, we took the train west. Stopping at a station in the Dakotas, my eyes dazzled as the conductor took me to see the Indians dance on the platform, dark red skin, wearing feathers, beating drums and chanting in a different type of rhythm and voice, like in the cowboy films, only different, this was real. Arriving in Helena, Montana we were met at the station by Andrew. He was tall and strong. Always had a smile, dark hair, big powerful hands. I remember how he rescued me one day. We were walking in the woods when in a sudden rush, Andrew pulled me up and jumped back. I had wandered into a snake pit. A few days later he came rushing at me again, picked me up and ran; a black bear apparently had more than a mild interest in us.

Back in Astoria, I spent most of my days with my friends, Walter Besendorfer and Emile Nemeckay—we were known as the Three Musketeers by all the neighbors. Walter's German father, a baker, lived quietly with the neighbor's "looks" as the war in Germany ended and a peace evolved. Emile's Czechoslovakian mother was an opera singer and actress at the old Paramount Studios a few blocks away—before the studio moved to Hollywood and the buildings became the barracks for the soldiers of the Army Post Office. I can still hear the troops marching under my window to the APO located near the Long Island Rail Road tracks, singing *Roll Out the Barrel.*

By 1954, a year after the ceasefire in Korea, I was just starting college; not fully understanding this new era, but I could feel an itch under my teenage feet. I walked on, supported only by the confidence of youth and dreams of going to college. From my education at Brooklyn Technical High School, where I drew and painted easily, I was praised for my book cover designs, I knew I wanted a career as an industrial designer and was told I would qualify. It was the era of Eisenhower and we didn't question too much.

I was interested in my baseball team and attending to the day in high school. I entered Brooklyn Tech, looked straight ahead and took one step at a time, one opportunity after the other as it came to me.

Nonetheless, my career actually started in fourth or fifth grade at PS 166, I designed covers for my book reports. The assignment was simply to read books and write about them. A book report, but I decided my reports also needed covers. It just seemed appropriate. I can't tell you why. I just did it. My teacher, Mrs. Flynn, liked the covers so much that she put them up on the hallway bulletin boards. On display. She said I'd get extra credit if I read more books, so I made more book covers, the likes of *Robinson Crusoe, The Call of the Wild,* and *Tom Sawyer.* She displayed them all. I not only liked doing them but seeing them displayed as well. As a kid, I drew things. Many things. Mechanical things and buildings. Street scenes. There was always a pencil or crayon handy. I enjoyed figuring out how things worked and how to get things done.

Tucked away in my memory, I recall in 1948, acting the role of a grandfather in a school play, I was telling my grandchildren about the history of New York City, answering their questions, while on the stage of the school's auditorium, packed full of the parents of all the students. The play was produced at my elementary school commemorating the 50th anniversary of the city's consolidation of five boroughs into the Greater New York City. I would imagine there were similar performances in all public schools at this time.

Outside, the war in Europe and Asia had ended. New aggressions were warming up in Korea, the Middle East, East Germany and the Slavic states. I grew up during the war. Mom's family was living in Nazi-occupied Norway. That tension seemed ever present while American troops were marching beneath my 5th story apartment window from their barracks to the Army Post Office in Woodside. I remember blackouts and rationing gas and certain food. Recycling rubber tires and retreads. Dad peeling the silver wrappers from cigarette packages into silver balls for the war effort. I remember V-D Day. Then V-J Day with great jumping and cheering. This war had ended only five years before I entered high school. Five years before North Korea invaded South Korea.

When I was in Junior High School, PS 10, I applied to one of New York City's special high schools, took the difficult tests, passed and was admitted. Of the three schools—Bronx High School of Science, Stuyvesant and Brooklyn Technical High School—I chose Brooklyn Tech, probably because it seemed logical as my father was an electrical engineer and, besides, my friend, Walter, who was a year older and living down the block, was going there.

Every morning I took the GG subway to Brooklyn and Tech. I loved it. The teachers were smart and cheerful. The reading and lab work and drawings were interesting. In my second year, I had a variety of special electives to choose from as a major for my third and fourth year. In addition to College Preparatory, there was Aeronautical, Civil, Chemical, Electrical, Mechanical and Structural Engineering, Architecture and Industrial Design. Industrial design was fresh, new and dynamic. It touched on engineering and art and structures and architecture. Automobiles, furniture, office systems, office design, tools, typewriters, eventually computers, digital information systems, murals, book design, store design, information design, and on and on. All the things people needed and used. A world in front of me. I wanted to do it all. Eventually, I did it ... all.

Drawing, watercolor, sculpture, pottery was wrapped together in design. At Brooklyn Tech, I drew complicated mechanical drawings, turned clay pots on a wheel and studied the sciences of production. I painted meticulous watercolor renderings—renderings were the "in" graphics in advertising at that time. Soon, it would be photography and typography. Today my watercolors are very quick, catching the essence of what I see or feel, with color and movement and flowing water.

I was offered a special choice to take a couple years of English classes with a teacher and two other students broadcasting on Tech's radio station WNYE atop the school in downtown Brooklyn. WNYE had a full educational program in all subjects from English through Math and Science helping infirmed and challenged New York City students to learn while at home and achieve a high school diploma. It was an honor. I spent an hour a day on radio.... talking with the teacher and two other students about a book, its plot or a character, a poem or a particular English problem like words that are spelled the same but have different meanings, led by my teacher, Miss Cowan. She was sharp and very clear about how we spoke and explained things. The minute I heard a recording of me on the first program, I hated the way I sounded. No, it wasn't the *deez, dems* and *does* of a Brooklynite of that time. I just didn't sound like what I heard in my head. I listened to people around me and on the radio and changed the way I spoke. I changed whatever rubbed me wrong such as saying "York" with a long "or" and adding a "u".... "Yurok".

During those years, I became familiar with the names of the leading designers, the originators of industrial design: Raymond Loewy, Henry Dreyfuss, Walter Dorwin Teague. Mr. Loewy seemed to be the most prominent, so I wrote him a letter explaining I was about to enter this field of study and asked him about his work. I was invited to his office by Elizabeth Reese (as I recall, Mr. Loewy's publicist), and was given a private tour. I don't think I actually met the Master. But I saw him. He was discussing the design of an ocean liner and pointing to parts of a large model, the famous *United States*. He seemed distinguished, dressed very well and had a generous face. I didn't realize then, I would get to know him in a few years. And few years after that, I would get to know Henry Dreyfuss as well.

I graduated from Brooklyn Tech in 1954, the year after the truce in Korea was negotiated between the North Koreans and the United Nations forces. I was thirteenth in my class of a thousand or more students, awarded the All City Art Medal, plus the balance of a small stipend, sponsored by a donor at Brooklyn Tech and a half-tuition New York State Regents Scholarship. I had applied to Syracuse University, Cincinnati and Pratt Institute and accepted in all three. Somehow, I was also selected for the All City All Star baseball team and played a game at the historic Ebbets Field, home of the Brooklyn Dodgers. Korea was heavy in the wind and I was intent on college.

I decided to stay at home to save the living expenses by choosing Pratt Institute, the legendary highly acclaimed art and design school in Brooklyn. A lucky *lucky* choice. Lucky, initially because while at Pratt, I learned the Syracuse industrial design curriculum folded. Lucky, mostly because I would meet and study with Rowena Reed, the noted teacher of design and three-dimensional relationships; she and the rest of the faculty taught me how to absorb the art of design and life's values that would guide my future and the decisions I make today.

Rowena Reed taught Three-Dimensional Design in the Industrial Design Department at Pratt. She'd helped establish the curriculum years before. At first, I felt she was a terror. I could never do anything without her moving this or that or changing one thing or the other during the "crits."; she would invariably say, it needed more work, the turning of an angle or enlarging a "dominant" movement in an early exercise in the class. Soon, I found most everyone felt the same way. And no matter what I was working on—an exercise of a series of lines in a wire structure or three static planes in space—there was always room for improvement. Always! Design was tough. How do I know what to change and how much? It went on like that for the three years after the Foundation year, until I graduated. It would go on throughout my entire career—I had absorbed Miss Reed's manner of teaching, and undoubtedly sometimes drove my design staff crazy.

When I went back to Pratt in 1963 for a graduate degree, after leaving the military, Miss Reed had become Chair of the Department. (She was called "Miss Reed" and maintained that distinction from her husband and partner, Alexander Kostellow. It was only later, after she retired that she became known as Rowena Reed Kostellow). She asked me to become her assistant and we became fast friends... but, I was still her student. Never would I hear, "Good!" or "That looks great, Louis"—except when I helped her with some management task in administering the department.

Pratt Institute was, "in its heyday," the leading design school in the country in education and influence within the profession. Particularly the Industrial Design Department. Numerous large corporations supported the department with generous donations (General Motors and Monsanto among others) largely because of the imagination and brilliance of Alexander Kostellow and Rowena Reed, the founders of the curriculum in the department (the structure of visual relationships), and its many fine instructors.

A good portion of my class at Pratt in 1954 were Korean War vets. They had a clear view of where they wanted to go, pulling up the standard for the entire class to the benefit of us all. They were also creative, had more life experience, having witnessed so many things. Years later, I would better understand this mysterious war and its veterans because of my friendships with the Korean Vets during these years.

The draft was still active, and I enrolled in ROTC, incurring a two-year service obligation so my education would not be interrupted. I joined Pershing Rifles, a military society within ROTC; in the final year, I became the regimental commander of Pratt's Corps of Cadets while I pushed on with my design studies of form and color, at the same time starting to understand the psychological and physical needs of people. I learned to use the tools of a designer—lines, planes and volumes; dominant, subdominant and subordinate movements; color and light; metaphor and meaning of symbols in culture and society; all while studying military history and customs.

In the summer of 1957, senior ROTC students attended Summer Camp at Fort Bragg near Fayetteville in North Carolina. Early on a bright sunny morning in June, about 25 of us from Pratt embarked with bag and baggage on a train from Penn Station, heading south to Fayetteville for 6 weeks of field training and barracks living. With the clatter of the rails, our chatter, jokes, questions and getting to know each other filled the long day. Until this trip, I had not been south of Route 46 in New Jersey. Never been to Maryland, Delaware, Washington DC, Virginia, nor the Carolinas. Arriving at the Fayetteville station I looked for a men's room. A door with a title above said WHITE. Next to it was another door labeled COLORED. I remember it looked uncomfortably shorter; someone would have to bend way-over to enter. I was shocked! Is this how people are treated here? This is a threatening message.

It's 1957 and I would not know the depth of racial hostility in this country for years to come. In 1948, President Truman signed an equal treatment and opportunity executive order and desegregated the US military; racial segregation in Kansas schools was addressed with Brown vs. Board of Education in

1954; Montgomery Bus Boycott happened 2 years ago; with Little Rock school desegregation in 1957. President Eisenhower signed the Civil Rights Act of 1957. Not all states and towns abided. Who would know what changes, wounds and deaths were eventually to come... in 3 years, Greensboro NC lunch counter sit-ins hit the news; Freedom Riders in 1961 resulted in horrific violence; the March on Washington in 1963; in 1964 voter registration in Mississippi and the Bloody Sunday March in Selma, AL; a Civil Rights Act and Voting Rights Act passed by Congress in 1965; and a broader Civil Rights Act in 1968 was signed by President Johnson. Yet, it will still take years—many more years to overcome racial discrimination.

Thinking back, I may have been split between going into the service as a commissioned officer and wanting to be a designer. Two divergent paths, one toward a career in design and one toward the military; individuality on one hand, teamwork on the other; creative thinking or uniformity; peace or war (although perhaps not an active war but an active pursuit to maintaining a peace.) As I think back, the decision I made was a logical next step. I had grown up during the Depression and WWII, was raised with a feeling of patriotism, a sense of obligation to serve my country—which may seem old fashioned today.

With my graduation, some changes were about to happen—my entry into the service and undoubtedly leaving New York for an assignment somewhere in the military. This also meant leaving home. Pratt was basically a commuter college in those years, and I was commuting from home. For a number of years, I was seeing Jeanne Caffrey, a friend of my friend Walter's girlfriend. Jeanne was studying to be a biochemist with plans for graduate school. During this past year of graduation, we seemed to be moving to a more solid bond at some future time. For now, I'd be away in the Army, while Jeanne finished her studies in New York.

When I graduated, I was designated a Distinguished Military Graduate in ROTC and offered a Regular Army commission with a three-year service obligation, not just the traditional two-year active duty Reserve Army commission. I accepted it. There was a Cold War in progress and the late fifties was a time of contradictions that would become evident in the drama of the sixties. The Korean War was in a ceasefire and not really settled. I did think it out and sensed there would be advantages coupled with that extra year obligation. Every one of these choices would greatly help me later.

A month after graduation I was a brand new 2nd Lieutenant, temporarily stationed at Fort Dix, New Jersey as a basic training cadre officer. The first thing I learned from my company commander Captain Truesdale, a tall kindly man, was, "Make the decision. Just make it!" This was to be one of the most important suggestions I would learn. A couple months later, I was in the Basic Officers Leaders Course in Fort Knox, Kentucky, the US Army Armor School, just outside of Louisville, Kentucky. I was placed in with the West Point Class. Each of them, a specimen of muscle and an expert in 100+ push-ups. Runners all. As for me, having spent the previous four years as a design student, I found myself spending weekends on the drill field getting into shape running around the track and doing push-ups. Because of the West Pointers, the minimal passing athletic requirements for our class were raised by 20%. And I needed to pass that. With lots of sweat and groans, I made it through those months and learned how to start being an officer, and about firing guns, driving and directing big M48 tanks and understanding how and why to use them.

I moved on to Fort Benning, Georgia, as a platoon leader in the 69th Armor Regiment of the 2nd Infantry Division and an owner of four M48 tanks. I took an aerial observer's course, learned how to identify tanks, howitzers and troop sizes (platoon and company size units) from different altitudes and distances. One day, I was out for practical training. I took off as an observer in a small bubble H-13 Bell helicopter. This was most special, the first time in a helicopter. The pilot brought the craft to a hover, tipped the nose slightly down. We started to move forward and then rise, going higher. Within a few feet, the whole world opened in front of me, a panoramic horizon I hadn't seen before... my mouth agape and a gleam in my eye, a most glorious experience. This is what I needed to do. I applied for flight school. Late in the summer of 1959 I said goodbye to Lieutenant Mizelle, my tank company commander, and entered the 3rd class of newly formed helicopter flight instruction for commissioned officers at Camp Wolters, Texas, learning to fly in the H-23 Hiller helicopter, a two-seat bubble design.

Jeanne and I were married in New York in May 1959, eleven months after graduation, sooner than I thought we would and a few months after I had arrived at Fort Benning, Georgia. I drove home for the ceremony. I hadn't seen Jeanne for almost a year and, understandably, I had the jitters. Although we had written frequently and spoke on the phone, I was nervous. I couldn't put my finger on why. Yet, I was coupled with feeling special. I had decided to dress in my Army white uniform—the only time I wore it as I recall. We were married at Trinity Lutheran Church and had a small reception with family in Forest Hills. The morning after the ceremony, we packed the car and drove down to Fort Benning, taking the scenic route along the Skyline Drive and the Blue Ridge Mountains. After a few months, with new orders in my hands, we moved to Flight School in Texas; a direct drive west from Fort Benning, Georgia, into Alabama, not to mention the state of Mississippi, into Louisiana, through Dallas, then Fort Worth, ending in Mineral Wells, Texas and Camp Wolters. Jeanne and I were getting along pretty well, surprisingly with the shift from living separately to living together in a military environment and now moving again. I asked Jeanne about this time and she replied, "Do you think I really remember what I was thinking when you were in Fort Benning? All I remember is we didn't have enough money to eat well and yet we had to get your uniforms starched and pay the officers' club dues. At the officer's wives' coffees, the Colonel's wife lecturing we wives that officers' wives didn't work."

Perhaps all these changes were a little difficult to handle but we worked them out. I soloed at Camp Wolters, completed this stage of flight training, then packed our bags and again moved, this time back East to advanced instruction flying the H-34 Sikorsky at Fort Rucker, Alabama. The road was the same route driving to Camp Wolters, except we diverted south for a day or two in New Orleans and Mardi Gras. The H-34 was the workhorse of the fleet. It carried 18 passengers plus crew, powered by a large B-17 type radial engine (R-1820 84) in the nose. I was one of the first commissioned officers (the third class as I understood) in the US Army to solo a helicopter. I earned my wings, graduating in June 1960. While I was learning to fly, I believe Jeanne was longing to find the right job—but where?

Helicopters were a new and significant service in the Korean War, used for reconnaissance and medical evacuation as we all learned from looking at *M*A*S*H*. The H-13 Bell helicopters along with the H-19 Sikorsky, saved the lives of thousands wounded in Korea. Seven years after the Korean truce, the "Huey," Bell HU-1A was introduced in March 1960 and would soon prove strategically significant in the course of the Vietnam War, armed with awesome firepower as well as serving as a troop transport and providing medical evacuation for many at a time. The Huey became the stepping-stone to technologically more highly advanced helicopters and "gunships." But Vietnam was not happening as yet... as far as we knew.

Out of flight school, I was assigned to the historic 3rd Armored Cavalry Regiment at Fort Meade, Maryland. We drove north, moved into a garden apartment in Laurel, Maryland. Gratefully, Jeanne had found a good position working in the research labs of W. R. Grace & Co. I was now Executive Officer of the Aviation Company, working for Commanding Officer Major William P. Hennessy. I found the local medical evacuation unit at Fort Meade had received a shipment of these new marvels early in 1961—the "Huey." Here I was able to "boot-leg" time and instruction from the Warrant Officer pilots in this unit. It was only eight years since the fighting in Korea had ended and a few of these chaps had flown there. I could see the skill in their eyes and their touch on the controls. In a few short months we became friends. This spectacular new chopper was the most advanced and powerful helicopter ever— you could pull up on the "collective stick" and go straight to 10,000 feet in what seemed a heartbeat. I had logged eight hours flying the Huey—needing two hours more to qualify as certified to fly the HU-1A.

But, something unexpected happened. Something big. The Soviets built the Berlin Wall. In October that year, President Kennedy ordered me and 40,000 others to West Germany—the 82nd Airborne Division, the 101st Airborne Division and the 3rd Armored Cavalry Regiment along with a few others, all STRAC I units, all ready to go at the drop of a hat. Suddenly, I had entered an impending Hot War in the midst of this Cold War—this new war had started in 1945 wth the partition of Germany into the East Zone (Soviet Union control) and the Southwest (British control), South (US control), Northwest (French control), as well as the city of Berlin itself, located in the middle of East Germany. Yalta and Potsdam in 1945, at least to Roosevelt, Churchill and Stalin, were the places where the Powers sliced up countries—Poland, Germany, Korea, the list goes on—leaving the real issues to be solved in another day.

I now was about to have six big H-34 helicopters under my command, newly assigned with their crew chiefs. I'd be picking them up from Fort Hood, Texas; then spend precious days with my team flying to various bases in the United States getting the radio crystals changed to European frequencies and other modifications for the European Theater, eventually seeing them delivered to Biloxi, Mississippi, cocooned for protection against the ocean spray and onto a ship for the trip across the Atlantic to Bremerhaven, West Germany. Without anyone saying it, but many thinking it, we could be moving into a danger zone in Europe. A Hot Zone, but not yet in combat. It was a stressful time and not much of it spent home with Jeanne. She must have been scared to death with the uncertainty and the news in the papers and on TV of the Berlin Wall. Months later I will hear of helicopters being shot at in Berlin, the news being suppressed from the papers. Jeanne never mentioned anything, saying she'd be fine, would go back to New York, live with her mother, finish her degree and probably find a position, as it turned out with the Institute for Muscle Disease.

Finally, I was able to drive Jeanne to her mother's apartment, get her settled. On that silent, evening drive to New York, somewhere along the New Jersey Turnpike, Jeanne, with all the accumulated pressure and uncertainty suddenly went blind. She couldn't see the road, nor the future. Fright. I didn't know what to do, other than pull over and talk. What do you do if your wife suddenly goes blind? I wondered if we should have searched for a hospital, but it was night and we were so close to New York. Eventually, we continued driving. Thankfully, Jeanne recovered in a few hours. Much later I found out this incident was the result of a migraine. I also wondered if our troubles had begun that very moment.

The next day I boarded the USNS *General Simon B. Buckner* in Baltimore, bound for Bremerhaven, and then on to Neubrücke and Hoppstädten Airfield, where I would fly helicopters and miss my wife.

A few months later, flying near the Rhine River, I was surprised to hear over the ship's radio the names of my warrant officer friends in the medical evac unit; naming each one individually, all in the clear, to return to base. Most unusual! Back at my base at Hoppstadten, I immediately called to see what had happened. Those pilots—my friends—had received orders to immediately deploy to Vietnam, directly, without returning first to the States. Mystified, I faced the next day's mission, my friends and "Nam" passing into yesterday as I attended to that day's assignment flying to Stuttgart, West Germany.

Vietnam was a country far, far away . . . as distant as Korea . . . and the majority of us had no idea what was happening there; it wasn't in the news. The Berlin Wall was. It was only years later that I shuddered, realizing how fortunate I had been to not have those two more hours for a 10-hour Huey check-out qualification. I had been the Aviation Company Executive officer and now Combat Unit Commander, critically desired job classifications (Aviation Unit Commander). I was qualified to fly and instruct pilots in the H-34, a large 18 passenger helicopter. The US Army did not fly the H-34 in Vietnam. The Marines flew the H-34 there. The Army was flying the Vertol H-21 (the "Flying Banana), later the larger Chinook and now the Huey—if 10 hours qualified me in the HU1A Huey, in all probability I would have been on my way to Vietnam at a time when the life expectancy of a helicopter pilot was measured in twenty minute segments of flying time. I had an angel on my shoulder.

We were the only aviation unit at Hoppstädten Airfield in Neubrucke. It was a peaceful area, green grass and hills nearby. The town had a US Army hospital and officer's quarters close by. The headquarters of the 3rd Armored Cavalry Regiment was in Baumholder, a much larger town a few miles east and a short flight to pick-up the regimental commander or others of his staff. Baumholder was a large military base teaming with troops and units moving in and out in rotation to the front lines of Soviet East Germany and Czechoslovakia, some in support missions to the combat ready units. It soon would be the largest military base in Germany. I never spent any time there but was told it was the "pits." Probably because of the confusion of the buildup and the shift in the strategy of US Forces in West Germany. But, that's only a guess.

With this new uncertain time, a new era of literary intrigue evolved with spies and stories of intrigue brought to us by writers lead by Graham Greene and John le Carré who with George Smiley, Alec Leamas, Harry Lime, Alden Pyle and books like *The Spy Who Came in from the Cold* would engross each of us. A new scene of real life emerges as we look into this new culture of conspiracy between the CIA and MI6 courting the KGB, all entangled within the Cold War, some hiring ex Nazi SS officers to run their intelligence . . . lasting until 1989 with the destruction of the Berlin Wall and the demise of the Soviet Union. But now, I was serving in this curiously real and charged atmosphere. Yet, those novels of the Cold War soon became real war stories from Vietnam by David Halberstam, Neil Sheehan and others. These writers shifted from the intrigue of Vienna and Berlin to fresh headlines from Saigon and Hanoi and as the years moved on, stories from Lebanon, Tehran and Baghdad. Seoul, Korea and the Far East will join in the mix of international intrigue and adventure. The faces coming off the pages of those novels and the faces of the senior soldiers surrounding me in Germany were real, as present today as one would see in the Korea of 1953. Many were sergeants, some master sergeants. Many had served in Korea, the lines in their face showing their time. Their eyes tell their story. They stayed in my memory for years. All distant, sometimes forgotten, but very, very present.

In Germany, I occasionally had wonderful special dinners at a local gasthaus, dining on *Spiessbraten,* a savory meat roasted with a special rich sauce, served at long family tables at the end of a road in the hills nearby. Other times I had simpler meals in the officer's dining room in our quarters, frequently wiener schnitzel. I remember seeing rosy-cheeked children playing on the streets of Birkenfeld, the town nearby, in front of walls still showing the pockmarks of machine-gun fire and chipped corners from the tank columns of World War II, sixteen plus years earlier. I was shocked to meet people who reminisced that things had been better under Hitler!

In early April 1962, Jeanne and I arranged a week in Paris. We'd been exchanging letters about every day or so, and we hadn't seen each other for about five or six months. I looked forward to a romantic rendezvous in Paris, took a night train, arrived at Gare de l'Est early one morning. A Citroën taxi to the hotel. The room wasn't ready as yet, so I left my bags and decided to see the city. I walked Boulevard Haussmann to des Italiens and the Place de l'Opéra, stopped for a croissant and coffee somewhere, continued to La Madeleine and Place de la Concorde, up the garden and the Champs-Élysées to the Arc de Triomphe, over to the Seine and down past the Louvre to Notre Dame, eventually back to the hotel. Seems I did this walk in about three or four hours.

Jeanne was due at Orly the next morning. I was awakened with a breakfast tray filled with a large cup and a pot of strong coffee, brioche and preserves from room service, found transportation to the airport, met Jeanne with a big hug, smiles, kiss and laughter. Our reunion was truly idyllic and most special. We had a grand week walking along the Paris streets, through Montmartre, Brancusi's studio at the Musée d'Art Moderne, seeing Van Gogh's

Sunflowers at the head of the stairs in the Jeu de Paume. Gendarmes carrying short machine guns were on street corners throughout the city reminding us of the Algerian War and the 1961 massacre. Still, Winged Victory, Mona Lisa at the Louvre, the Eiffel Tower and a myriad other glories carried us. It was as though we were drifting through my picture books, each well-known photo and painting from my art history courses had come alive, even a walk through an Utrillo poster I had hanging from my old apartment in New York. One evening I had fish, for what seems the first time, moist and flavorful, it even looked delicious—at a delightful restaurant off the Champs-Elysees. So different from the fish when I was growing up.

My hair was short in those days, but I was never taken for a GI, mostly for a Brit. Best I could figure after mentioning it to others is that the English come to Paris in the spring, and it was now spring with Easter to follow. In a second it was time to leave. Jeanne flew back to New York, me on a train to Neubrucke and my bachelor quarters. My first wife and I parted, sure that we would be coming together again soon.

About 20 klicks (kilometers) north from Neubrucke is a charming small town of well-kept shops, Idar-Oberstein. I walked into one, beautifully designed and constructed of polished wood, owned by a local jeweler. I spoke with the owner and marveled at the green stones in the case, soon to become familiar with the beauty and price of an emerald. I was enchanted with its glistening shift of light and color as you moved the stone. Seems more I was longing to get back to my career as a designer. That being the case, I put in papers to resign my commission.

Throughout the fall the skies were gray; the weather seemed to rise from the ground, creating an impenetrable fog that we would carefully inch through, flying low, straining to see beyond, keeping the road below visible. Helicopters didn't have radar then—or rather, the ones I was flying didn't. I gained life experiences during my time in Germany . . . talking a depressed senior sergeant through a cut wrist, near suicide; flying over eastern France and seeing the craters left by World War I shelling; and learning of the obstinate independence of French flight traffic control, who responded to an English request in high speed unintelligible French . . . repeatedly. At least to an American ear. Mostly, I learned from my non-coms, my senior sergeants, flight crew chiefs and tank commanders, loaders and drivers. A few were Korean era vets who had a knowing look in their eyes, each a portrait of service.

While I was an instructor checking out another pilot, Chuck Jolley, a dear friend, in demonstrating a difficult training maneuver . . . a 180° low level autorotation (a power off landing with a turn into the wind) . . . my timing in cutting power and initiating the turn was a microsecond off. Immediately increasing rpms and pulling in power, I experienced a very hard landing. Luckily, the ship bounced to a hover. I could see from the shadow cast by the setting sun, the landing gear of my big H-34 was severely damaged, hanging at a curious angle, the antenna wires limp and dragging under the fuselage. My crew chief, a senior sergeant who was on the ground, thought he saw the situation, and with hand signals motioned I should land. I shook my head, "No!" He repeated, I pointed down. Finally, moving both hands to the side of his head, opened his mouth and widened his eyes and ran to rally the troops to make a cradle with mattresses from their barracks. Without the exchange of words and pure eye contact and hand gestures, the plan was for me to hover the helicopter over the mattresses and set the damaged helicopter into the cradle. We never practiced this procedure . . . and it would be a tricky maneuver; the helicopter, being tall and narrow, and now without horizontal support, could easily tip over sideways. The cradle, as soft as the mattresses are, would have to provide enough lateral support. I hovered for some time for the cradle to be assembled. The time seemed excruciatingly long, and the effects of the jarring landing amplified by high stress in the realization of no landing gear began to play on Chuck's nervous system. I was busy holding the aircraft in a hover. Chuck started to shake, physically. Uncontrollably it seemed. What to do? I turned over the controls to him. Instantly, he steadied. Then, I started shaking. We shifted controls a number of times until we both steadied. Now the cradle was finally completed, I eased the ship over my future support, watching and responding to hand signals from my crew chief. I lowered the helicopter until I felt resistance. We were now supported in the cradle, with the rotors giving stability. I decided to pressure the tail, right and left to make sure I was solidly fixed in place, lowered the collective so our full weight was in the cradle, still keeping the engine in power. I felt the ship tip slightly to the left . . . my heart jumped to my throat . . . but it held. Heavy breathing. I started to slowly reduce engine power and rpm. We held our breath. If we tipped more, we'd have precious little time or power to immediately go to a hover. The rotors slowed and I held what breath I still had. Wanting no sudden jolts to unbalance the aircraft, I did not brake the rotors. They finally slowed to a stop . . . I looked at Chuck, I think he smiled, I then cut power. Finally, it was quiet. I could feel my heart beating. Perhaps I heard it.

Lucky. Lucky. Lucky. I gratefully thanked my troops, many who spent the night without a mattress.

By 1962, short of five years in the Army—one year and a few months of them on active duty in West Germany—I received orders to return to the States for my discharge. But the Cuban Missile Blockade had surfaced. President Kennedy and Premier Khrushchev were in serious discussions. War seemed near. The Navy was extended (meaning, no changes in station assignment, nor discharges allowed). Then the Air Force was extended. Not yet the Army. My first orders back to the States were to be a Troop Commander on a troop ship. That was cancelled. The next order was to fly home to New York. That, too, was cancelled. Curiously, I was promoted to Captain while this was going on . . . all within 2-3 weeks of each other. And then I received another order to return by air. It stuck, and in late October 1962, I was in Frankfurt on a jet to McGuire Air Force Base in New Jersey and finally landed home, Jeanne and my folks meeting me. Jeanne and I rejoined our marriage and within months, I restarted my design career and entered graduate school—again at Pratt Institute.

⁂

After all these years as a designer, no one has ever asked me about the wisdom to serve in the Army for so long. If they did, I would gratefully say that being in the service not only allowed me to learn to fly, but also to fly a new emerging aircraft that would change the face of air accessibility—apart from the military—for many industries and rescue services. "Vertical Takeoff and Landing Aircraft" became my graduate thesis at Pratt. Nevertheless, beyond this subject, the Army helped me to better understand how people make decisions, how they perform under stress, how they find their way, and how I could use creative and intelligent criteria to enhance "wayfinding" as it emerged into a new sector of Information Architecture and Design, not to mention navigating the emerging complexities of product and space development and specialist team management.

Wayfinding, simply stated, is comprised of signs and symbols, providing travelers with needed information and reassurance that they were going in the right direction to get to their destination. Three-dimensional maps help them visualize where they are in their journey and how much farther they need to go. In other words, as I said once in an interview for a major design program for Boston's Logan Airport, "I help people find their way." Lots of laughter around the table. (We were awarded the project!)

With this skill, I collaborated with the New York City Subway system as it expanded under tough financial times, and similarly, with New York City's LaGuardia and Kennedy airports, as well as Boston's Logan Airport Master Information & Wayfinding Plan, all making life easier for travelers.

My military service gave me a base in creative management to run my projects on-time and in-budget; to understand and develop the skills of leadership; to recognize the primary focus of attention needed at the moment; to make sure the tasks I was doing and directing my team were safe and needed; to be able to grasp the needs of a variety of people from all walks of life, from different cultures; and to deal with any amount of stress with equanimity. Coupled with my education at Pratt, I could design anything. And I just about have!

This experience certainly was a key benefit in my working with the Korean War Veterans Memorial Advisory Board—comprised of two four-star generals, one with a Congressional Medal of Honor, and ten distinguished members from the Army, Marines, Air Force, the majority with the rank of Colonel—who were clearly comfortable with me as a former Army Captain!

I had spent my active duty time with talented American veterans, some serving in the Korean War. Tank gunners, helicopter crew chiefs and pilots. I got to know their skills and their concerns, their needs and their spirit. All part of my time in the military and years later, when I felt they would form the theme of one of the important projects of my career . . . thirty years later. They, together with my design office staff, the men and women of all cultures and talents in management and leadership, possessing design skills in space, communications, product, packaging and wayfinding straegy; who together with my special consultants in writing, psychology, anthropology and humanity allowed me to complete an array of programs affecting the lives of millions.

With my master's degree in hand, in 1964 I was offered a lead position in the Corporate Design Department of Corning Glass Works. My first job title was Architectural Designer and then Director of Exhibit Design for Corning throughout the States and in Europe. I was hired by Davis Chiodo, a dynamic Princeton-educated architect and head of the Department of Architectural Design, and a joy to work with. I made the right decision. I designed exhibits and facilities for all the various divisions at Corning and rapidly moved up, working directly on design strategy with the CEO of each major division—Consumer Products, Electronic, Chemical, Research and New Product Development; it was an extraordinary opportunity for a starting post. It was as if starting at the very top.

Jeanne and I moved to Corning, New York, found an apartment in a small home in Painted Post, a mile from Corning. I wondered if this was going to be a place Jeanne would find comfortable. It would take me a few months to realize that was only a fond hope. What would she do in Corning, where would she work? These were hard questions and we tried to work through them, however Jeanne soon found a position at Cornell University working for Dr. Robert Holley deducing the cloverleaf secondary structure of t-RNA (a proof of the Watson and Crick double helix as Jeanne explained), a worthy opportunity and initial step to enter graduate studies in biochemistry. It was near impossible in those years for a woman to find a graduate school entry position in scientific studies. She spent most of her time at Cornell while I was working at Corning or traveling on business. Dr. Holley was to receive a Nobel Prize for this work, and Jeanne had worked with him on this path.

In mid 1966, I designed new exhibitions for Corning's Corning Ware/Pyrex and Centura's booths at the January 1967 National Housewares Exhibit at McCormick Place in Chicago, the country's largest convention center. I created a new direction for that year's annual exhibition, worked closely with Corning's renowned product design consultant, Sara Little. It was a splendid design. As a topper, I retained Peter Max to develop a dynamic centerpiece animated puppet show. Peter was becoming a counterculture icon known for brilliant colors and alluring patterns. By mid-January 1967, both exhibits, Corning Ware and Centura, were installed and would be "showstoppers." Early on the morning of Monday, January 16th at 2:05 am, a fire burst out at McCormick Place. It was out of control by the time firefighters arrived. Despite being thought fire-proof, by 9:50a.m. the McCormick Place roof collapsed. No one was ever to see these Corning exhibitions, nor the puppet show.

Later that year I received a telephone call asking if I wanted to be considered for a special position. Raymond Loewy, one of the legendary originators of the industrial design profession and whose office I had toured while in high school, had an opening in his Paris office. My interview was at his New York City residence on Fifth Avenue. I had practiced my minimal French pronunciation— "je ne parle pas français très bien"—and decided best to be clear and straight with Mr. Loewy, saying I knew very little French. He was most charming and, after talking a short time, straight out offered me the position of Director General, the head of his Paris office. He would put me through Berlitz's Total Immersion French language course. I received a confirmation letter. One week before I was to give notice to Corning, Mr. Loewy called from France, most apologetically, and said that his French colleagues did not want another American as their director. Instead he wanted me to meet Bill Snaith, his partner in New York, to see if I could fit in the Park Avenue office. However, that didn't seem to work out. I met Snaith, but I guess he had other plans. Later I found out that he and Mr. Loewy weren't getting along. I never had a chance to tell Mr. Loewy I had toured his office when I was a young high school student.

I took a couple of telephone meetings—one from the West Coast offering me to bring new life to the *Queen Mary* post-voyage life as a hotel/tourist attraction, and another that led to a face-to-face meeting in New York with a design consultancy. These enabled me to see that greater opportunities exist. I passed on the *Queen Mary* opening, and in 1968, moved from Corning back to New York City to join Robert Gersin in a design consultancy. Over a period of the next twelve years as Executive Vice President with Gersin I brought in and managed half the business.

In my years with Jeanne there had been long periods of separation, nearly a year when I was away before we were married, a year while I was in West Germany (family wasn't allowed by the military under critical assignments) and now most of the weeks were spent in different places during the three to four years at Corning. We grew apart, slowly, so much so that for many of those months I didn't realize how far apart we really had become. We took a special trip to an island in the Caribbean to see if we could mend what we had. We didn't talk much about it as we never really talk much about significant details and feelings, as I now realize. Probably, we each said things we shouldn't have. Seems we both wanted something else, something more. We were young and had high hopes for our relationship, but it was not working out. Sadly, we decided to separate when I took the new position in New York. In New York, I was a bachelor for a few years, sometimes licking my wounds over the break-up of my marriage, but mostly working on this new opportunity in my career. Slowly I began to date again and in 1969 met Sandra Balestracci, a ballet dancer with New York City Opera. She was charming and fun, and we decided to marry in November 1970 in San Francisco . . . we were both traveling. Once again, this lasted 4 or 5 years and we separated in 1974 or 75. I was happy, she said she wasn't. Dumbfounded, I started believing I couldn't trust my feelings; I sought help, while vowing to keep future relations simple and unattached. After a long separation, we mutually decided to divorce.

Why? How could this happen with both Sandra and Jeanne? I found a therapist; thought I was spending more time and attention to my work and my clients with less care to my marriage. Somewhat oversimplified, I admitted this and have apologized to both these splendid individuals. Jeanne had remarried, went to Johns Hopkins University, in 1973 earned a PhD in biochemistry, divorced at some time, joined the National Institutes of Health, obtained a senior position, eventually Chief of the Cardiovascular Sciences Initial Review Group at the Center for Scientific Review, now retired. Sandra remarried, continued her performances with the New York City Opera Ballet and other traveling companies, and ultimately with her husband opened a successful regional school of dance in Williamsburg, Virginia.

I have been married three times, first to a scientist, second to a ballerina, and now, a third time to the singer-songwriter, Judy Collins, who is my wife today. We met on a blind date, put together in 1978 by mutual friends, at an ERA (Equal Rights Amendment) fundraiser at the Ginger Man, renamed for that evening to the "Ginger Person", and had a splendid time talking to each other and our friends amongst the crowd and chatter, and many who came up to speak to Judy. When I escorted her home, Judy said she would be traveling in four days and away for a month or so. She called me on each of those four days. I was flying. On her return, our first real date was dinner at Orsini's on July 20, 1978. We were married in 1996, but from the very beginning, we knew this was real and we were instantly together. We've been together now for 42 years.

Henry Dreyfuss, the renowned industrial designer, chose me and my team to lead a series of major programs for one of his clients, AT&T, including a new retail strategy and the inaugural Annual Meeting for their new Chairman and CEO, John D. deButts. What prompted Mr. Dreyfuss to give me one of his clients, I will never know. Over the following four years, until his death, we would meet frequently at my office in New York, and at times downtown at 95 Broadway. It was an honored experience.

In April 1993 I was in the hospital for 10 days from a complication caused by a burst appendix, actually from a stomachache, that in reality was a partial untreated and undiagnosed bust appendix that abscessed a year earlier; and now a final painful burst that knocked me to the ground. Now, flat on my back as I awakened, I asked the nurse where I could have a cigarette. She looked at me with great concern, hesitated. I sensed a smile on her lips. I looked up from her eyes and saw the scene. Entering my body were many tubes hanging from bags hooked to a rolling post. There may have been two rolling posts. One bag was dripping Demerol. I was not feeling any pain from a long deep horizontal cut across my stomach, kept open by the surgeon, Dr. Leon Pachter, to heal from the inside out. I decided it impossible to struggle out of bed and shuffle down the corridor to the stairwell. I stopped smoking that instant... aided by Demerol.

Demerol. On one of the following days, I awakened in the middle of the night and looking north through my windows, seeing the lights of the city, I also saw a man crawling up the side of a building around the 25th floor, five or six blocks away. I clearly remembered this and drifted back to sleep. Another night, there were conversations going on down the hall and knowing this was a meeting I needed to attend, started pulling the tubes out of my body and removing the IV from my right hand, started struggling out of bed. Somehow a nurse appeared, stopped me and reattached everything. I have no idea what she said, and I was back out in dreamland.

Each morning Judy would be waiting at the door for visiting hours to start, her face beaming with a broad smile and great affection. At the appointed moment, she would be in the room, and we would talk as she rubbed my feet. Oh, how wonderful. I was waiting to see her. This morning, Judy was standing still at the door looking very serious. I was concerned, and as she came close to me, she said, "I think we should get married." I smiled and wanting to be light, said dumbly, "That won't" and as I'm saying these words, a cartoon cloud comes to light over me and I'm grabbing the emerging words, one by one, to gather them back . . . "stop me from dying." Groan. How dumb could I be?

*

Somewhere in these years, I sought out and was commissioned to develop the Master Plan for the new offices of the Department of Justice in Washington, DC; and a similar service for the new offices of the National Fire Protection Association in the Boston area. In 1979, I received the commission and organized the Food and Drug Administration design program for nutritional information on all American food packaging. We called it Nutrition Facts—and to this day, millions of consumers use this information 24/7. A colleague told me that conservatively, 4 million people in the United States use this information each hour. That's an amazing number. While traveling, I've seen a similar notice on food packages in the UK and in Germany. A couple years ago, my nephews gave me a special Christmas present, a snack package from Japan that has a likeness of the Nutrition Facts chart.

From a designer's view, my military service was a profound period of daily research. In one case, it provided me a foundation for designing aircraft instrumentation with tactile knobs—fulfilling a need to distinguish one knob from another by "feel," resulting in a different shape and appearance for each so that a pilot, flying blind or in rough weather can not confuse the knob that makes a radio frequency adjustment for another adjusting directional codes. In another case, my partner and I were commissioned to design a TWA 707 jet interior composed of new special features for a New York to Los Angeles all first-class service. We started the project, developed a number of splendid ideas, and there it sat, never to be built. That happens.

Head, a leading manufacturer of skis, became a client in the early Seventies. The industry was changing, and another group of consumers was emerging. With that understanding, I designed Head Ski out of its familiar all-black skis into a spectrum of color and light—brilliant red and oranges to lightning blue—each aligning with the proficiency of skiers and their personal choices, ushering in a new era of personal dynamics for this sport as a winter culture. My team and I designed and introduced a new panty hose product, an on-point inexpensive product sold in my now-famous orange vinyl pouch that brought a fashion look and feel to women at a very affordable price in the supermarket—especially when compared to the cost of stockings and panty hose in department stores. I gave it a name, No Nonsense. Within a few years No Nonsense was the singular branded product in the non-branded division of Kayser-Roth, enticing Gulf and Western to purchase Kayser-Roth Hosiery Company for a sizable amount.

By 1979, it was clear I needed a change. With much of our success, Bob Gersin had been managing his own projects, growing impossibly difficult. I heard many staff complaints. Bob and I talked but nothing changed. It would be a significant move; as for the last twelve years we had been deemed one of the top five design firms in the United States. I decided to leave the partnership in 1980 to open an independent practice with a fresh staff of designers, producing projects as varied as the editorial guidelines for IBM; programs for the National Fire Protection Association (I started Stop, Drop and Roll for fire safety while at Gersin); the dining area and restaurant at the Statue of Liberty—the largest fast-food restaurant in America; the AT&T communication technology exhibition at the Los Angeles Olympic Games; and the Wine Exhibition at the California Museum of Science and Technology (now the California Science Center). I was asked by Randy McAusland to serve on the Grants Committee for his Design Arts Program of the National Endowment for the Arts, and as committee leader for the presentation to the National Council during the contentious Mapplethorpe and Serrano period of Congressional funding challenges in the early 1990s. During this time, I received the commission to create the mural at the Korean War Veterans Monument. Several years later another project of international significance soon emerged, the design for the United Nations' Dag Hammarskjöld Medal for peacekeepers.

Over dinner in 1997, Karl "Rick" Inderfurth, a United States ambassador to the United Nations, mentioned there were no memorials or medals or other recognition given to peacekeepers killed while in service to humanity, these valiant soldiers from a variety of countries coming together to help nations in trouble by maintaining a peace in places as distant as Bosnia and Macedonia, Sudan and East Timor. Madeleine Albright, then the American Ambassador to the United Nations, had identified and taken up the cause, and with Rick, proposed to Kofi Annan to develop such a medal. The Security Council approved it, calling it the Dag Hammarskjöld Medal.

Dag Hammarskjöld, a Swedish diplomat, economist and author (his book "Markings" a spiritual work as I read it, tending to reflect a melancholy side of human emotions), was the second Secretary-General of the United Nations. He was killed in 1961 en route to ceasefire negotiations in the Congo; his plane went down in Northern Rhodesia (now Zambia). He was awarded the Nobel Peace Prize posthumously—the only person to be so awarded. President John F. Kennedy called Hammarskjöld "the greatest statesman in our century."

During the dinner discussion, I suggested the "medal" needed to be designed and volunteered to design it. Rick and Ambassador Albright were delighted, confirmed the commission with the UN and then with me. Trying to find meaningful symbols to feed my imagination, I ventured to the UN headquarters in Manhattan to see what I could see of the sculptures on the plaza and in the building's halls; and to the Metropolitan Museum of Art to look at the collection of armament and weapons of war, which reminded me of the guns I aimed when I was in the Army. Nada. I hit a blank. Finally, I had a talk with James Parks Morton, Dean at the Cathedral of St. John the Divine. Critical to our discussion were his thoughts of the strength and yet, fragility of human life. In Jim's words, I found inspiration and began to search for symbols to show that strength and fragility.

Of all the designs I've completed, the Dag Hammarskjöld Medal is the simplest, embodied with deep cathartic feelings. It recognizes the sacrifice of those men and women, military and civilian, who have lost their lives while serving in peacekeeping operations for the UN. It honors those who went to distant lands in search of peace, who were frequently exposed to situations where there was no peace to keep, who were confronted by a broad and great range of risks, and who bravely carried out their work with sensitivity, paying the ultimate price while serving under the United Nations flag. I was told no nation recognizes the loss of a life with a "medal." This medal will not be worn. It is given to the individual's mother, brother, spouse or child. It is designed as a tribute for the loss of a life and therefore a symbol of that life and a remembrance of it. It focuses on the quality of the life taken—not on their death. Nothing is more precious than a life.

I gave the medal an ovoid shape, which the mother or spouse or child of the lost peacekeeper could hold in their hand. The ovoid represents life, the form resulting from the chaos in the origin of the universe as the planets find their moving patterns around the sun; the form found in the creation of all life within a woman's body.

Made of clear crystalline glass, formed from the elemental attributes of nature—earth, air, water, fire. Crystal in the medal represents the beauty and purity of life, fragility as well as strength, all attributes inherent in the physical structure of the material and the symbolic meaning held through all cultures. Its form embodies the origins of values, underlying all existing religious and cultural symbols—emblematic of a higher source.

> *The core of life.*
> *The basics of life.*
> *The elements of life.*
> *The essence of life.*

The peacekeeper's name is engraved in the glass, along with the symbol of the United Nations, and the words "In the Service of Peace" and "The Dag Hammarskjöld Medal," written in English and in French—the UN Secretariat's two working languages. I wanted the tribute to cross all national boundaries, all cultures and all religions.

In recognizing those who have fallen, the ideas behind the Dag Hammarskjöld Medal is not dissimilar from those behind a memorial. As I walk around a monument, I become a part of it. It requires *me* to do so. It requires *you*. It needs the active contribution of the observer, as participant transcending their feelings by devoting the time to look. Without us there is no memorial.

⁂

I see what led to certain events in my life. I look ahead thinking I can see Tomorrow yet glance back to better understand how to deal with Today. With the blink of an eye, I gather more than a hint of the subject. The complicated intermix of senses, memory and intelligence gives me an immediate knowledge of what I survey. I begin to understand.

The plan I made in the early 1970s to stay unattached after my first and second marriages didn't work out after I met Judy Collins, my life partner. Jim Morton, Dean of the Cathedral of St. John the Divine, who had spoken so eloquently to me about the vulnerability of life, married us at high noon on April

16, 1996, It was a Tuesday and all our friends and family from near and far were there, including Madeleine Albright, Gloria Steinem, and on and on. Our sisters, Holly and Dorothy and nieces, Natalie and Corrina were bridesmaids and Judy's granddaughter Holly was the flower girl; our brothers Michael, Dave, Denver and brother-in-law, Harvey, nephews, Matthew and Joshua, and two close friends Mort and Rob were groomsmen. Judy's and my mom, dad and Judy's stepdad here with more family and friends filled the choir pews of the Cathedral. Judy sang "Wedding Song for Louis" to me and I recited a poem to her. We said our vows, Jim offered communion to all "who were breathing", gave us his blessing and we lead everyone from the Cathedral as trumpets and Irish bagpipes played. Judy and I giggled and skipped back to sign some papers, then off to Synod House across the garden under an umbrella and light shower for our reception. The New York Times featured the wedding. A life with Judy is undoubtedly the best decision I ever made.

Growing up, I took many things for granted. I didn't question what I saw. Why something was the way it was didn't raise an issue . . . yet. Somehow, I became concerned about how things looked and why things happen. The question "why" started to become apparent as I grew. Between entering Pratt and starting my profession, I questioned the reasons for a poorly designed classroom, why a doctor's examination rooms lacked clothing hooks, why a product screamed "look at me" when it should just simply be beautiful, working silently and reliably, and safely.

As I matured, I found myself walking down the street questioning why sidewalks were too narrow, why that storefront was so ugly, and why this new building entrance didn't really welcome people. So many things were mindless, and not right; I could not yet understand the joy surrounding me. I sought help and worked hard to not be so critical. I inherently trusted people, at least until I looked into their eyes and sensed if I should after a few expectations failed to materialize.

Lines, planes, and volumes still fill my life today. They are there in the underlying structure of how I think. Dominant. Sub-dominant. Sub-ordinate. Whether in stories, poems or music. They have become part of my design-thinking consciousness. A memorial to honor a time, a medal to remember the loss of a life, a digital tool to explain a city, a label to tell you what is healthy.

Today I fill a fair portion of my time reading books and articles. Research. Many of them are about the early days of my country. Some about design, science and art... and anything that I can get my hands on that reflects fresh ideas that can matter. And of course, now and still, today, Korea and other parts of Asia. In the morning, I read poetry—Billy Collins, Robert Bly, Wallace Stevens—one poem each morning. I wait for Bob Caro's next volume in the Lyndon B. Johnson biography. Or Ron Chernow's. It's impossible to keep up with my wife, Judy, who seems to devour books daily, play music, write songs, turn stories into books. I'm a slow reader. I try to stay abreast of the latest advances in materials and leave time for song and theater and dance because they make a difference. They matter.

There are eleven different types of linear curves that form part of the design vocabulary—neutral, accented, catenary, parabolic... you get the idea. Many products today use only one or two simple neutral curves. No excitement. No movement. No diversity. No accent or pushing a direction. Boring. Although not everything needs to be exciting, everything should be beautiful and have intrinsic meaning and value. At times to get there, I still do linear wire studies, three curves in space, and prop them up on a shelf, rotating them, making adjustments so they look great from all angles. My teacher, Miss Reed said it's a "warm-up." Positive and negative forms interwoven with the hopes and dreams of all ages in all the places of work and play and life. I seek to make my eyes sparkle, to marry how I feel and engage the smile I carry when walking through a museum. I don't have enough time for it all. But I try. I want it... enough time to find the right phone or car, the right office chair, the exhibit that tells you a clear story. The train that get you there comfortably, the doctor's dressing room with hooks to hang your clothes, a cup that just fits the hand, its edge touching the lips just so. A teapot should not drop a spot of tea. The back seat of a car has to have room for the top of your head. Simple things. Simple things that matter.

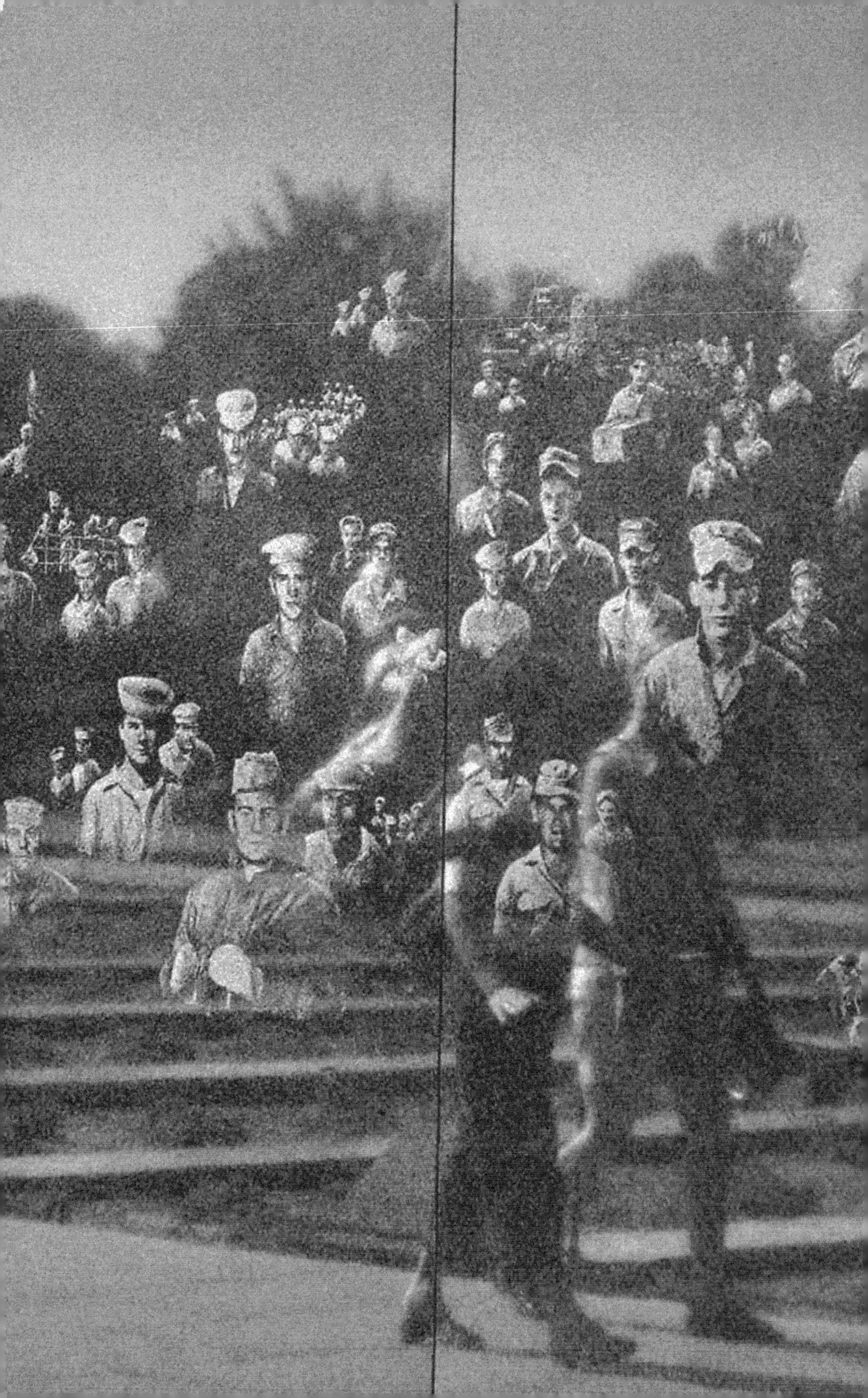

Its blood and bullets now on our minds
The times they never change that much

THREE
FACES IN THE MURAL

They needed to get out of there.

It was freezing cold in the North Korean mountains on the way to Chosin Reservoir. Worse, the Chinese Communists were there ahead of the Marines, hidden, waiting and far outnumbering the American and United Nations troops. When attacked, the Marines were losing men, killed each night. The situation seemed impossible. Roads were blocked and an isolated company was in bad trouble. They needed a break. Lt. Colonel Raymond Davis, answering the call from Major General Oliver P. Smith, lead his battalion in a rescue mission during a nightmare withdrawal from the Chosin Reservoir disaster, through the woods in radio silence, away from the paths and mountain roads, shielded in the stealth of a dead, dark frozen winter night. Just before dawn, Davis found the remaining soldiers of Company F and their Captain William Earl Barber. He relieved the beleaguered rifle company who was about to receive another searing, endless firefight from the Communist Chinese, in the process seized and opened the vital Toktong Pass, freeing the only route available for two isolated Marine regiments in danger of being cut off by "superior hostile forces" during their re-deployment to the Port of Hungnam.

~~

I pored over books about the war, examined photographs of as many wars as I could find, searching for the "look" of the soldiers. Chosin Reservoir was one of the first deadly battles in Korea. Once or twice I was awake in the middle of the night with images merging in my head. It was the early weeks of the

OPPOSITE: Faces in the Mural

project. I stared into thousands of eyes and began to see their innocence and their determination. The eyes of the soldiers in Korea had the same look of those I had seen in photographs from the Civil War and the First and Second World Wars. In the young men's eyes, I could see pain, yet energy and hope. I could almost sense the beating of their heart, the pulse of their courage.

The celebrated combat photographer David Douglas Duncan captured images of the Marines in Korea. In one, that blank look of despair showed the hopelessness of the situation. I was taken by the look of anguish in the eyes of those Duncan had photographed. As I started to visualize the mural, while some of the concepts were abstract images, most of them were figurative—about the people. This was unusual for me, because my work until then had been very abstract—very contemporary and three-dimensional. Certainly not representational.

I also looked at paintings of war and of protest—no less pertinent than photographs to memorialize events of a time. Picasso in 1951 painted *Massacre in Korea,* protesting the killing of North Koreans brought on by anti-Communist forces; and *Guernica* in 1937, the bombing of the city by Franco using German planes. George Bellows painted *The Germans Arrive* in 1918 showing the severing of a citizen's hands by the Hun. Édouard Manet in 1868, painted *The Execution of Emperor Maximilian,* and Francisco Goya commemorated the Spanish resistance to Napoleon's occupation during the Peninsular War, with *The Third of May 1808.* Each work of art brings a deep feeling of the horror of war, and its futility.

I was drawn once again to the Civil War photos of Mathew Brady, and as counterpoint the photographs of Paul Strand and Dorothea Lange, Walker Evans and Harry Callahan—all favorites of mine and all from another period in US history, not far removed from the 1950s, not faces of a shooting war but faces of a different sort of war, a time of struggle with poverty, with drought and dust storms of the 1920s and '30s. Portraits. W. Eugene Smith's *Juanita,* 1953, in black and white, captured the subject against a black background, her head tilted down to her left, her eyes quietly looking in the same direction, filled with a sense of her own resolve. I began to visualize a wall of portraits, all emerging from a length of dark gray granite; I decided the wall must be personal . . . and compassionate—an intimate reflection of those who had served, grounded with my own thoughts of this conflict and how it affected my life and formed those of so many others in the early '50s.

FACES IN THE MURAL

There are four classic ways of commemorating service—three were already present on the Mall. One is a representation of a great leader, and thereby, a remembrance of a tragic and bloody war. Certainly, that is Lincoln and the Civil War. Another, like the one in my old neighborhood square—yet not like that one at all—a list of names of the dead, an honor roll etched in black granite on the nation's square. That's the Vietnam Veterans Memorial. The third is a significant abstract symbol reflecting the individual, as is the obelisk for the Washington Monument. The fourth way, the most universal yet different and contrasting to the other three while touching the hearts of all families, is a reflection of the person, the individual, the people as in a photograph of a loved one, put in the place of honor at home, on your sideboard or your mantelpiece for all to see when you have visitors. This mural would be the *Nation's Mantelpiece*.

My concept for the wall would be composed of portraits of "American soldiers," men and women, taken by the many American military war photographers between 1950 and 1953 in Korea. Somewhere I sensed the stirring call in Aaron Copeland's "Fanfare for the Common Man", making the back of my neck shiver.

The repositories for military photographs are the National Archives, the Air and Space Museum, the Library of Congress as well as a few other locations near Washington, DC. I decided to recruit Linda Christenson, who lives near Washington to do the photo research. My senior graphic designer, Jennifer Stoller, would work with the team.

I gave Linda a specific list of occupations to find. She pulled selections of men and women, all cultures, from all the services, Army, Navy, Marines, Air Force and Coast Guard, in all jobs—truck drivers, mechanics, cooks, nurses, doctors, chaplains, gunners, armorers, ammo carriers, pilots, navigators, tank commanders and drivers, landing officers, engineers, construction and communications specialists, and more. Each would become a portrait unto itself, organized within the mural in groups of specialties in each of the branches of service.

Linda and her two professional photo researchers looked through tens of thousands if not hundreds of thousands of pictures at the National Archives and the Air and Space Museum and the Department of the US Navy, taken in Korea between 1950 and 1953. I had asked her to find faces looking straight into the camera, with the light coming from one direction (hopefully from their right—in my mind and on the wall, this would be from the east, over the Washington Monument—it would be the morning sun). I saw them as individuals, placed together as a group of thousands, faces that gave a sense of seriousness—"steadfast" was an apt description, but I kept searching for another word.

I presented the idea to the Advisory Board and proposed a number of concepts in which the men and women could be featured: some of them isolated or alone, others in a battle scene—cropped from photos, the details would be revealed as the viewer approached it; and some with excerpts of letters written home; or simply, faces by themselves. Portraits. Head and shoulders. I preferred to compose a series of portraits, showing men and women, all cultures, as they would report for their job. As simple as that. I explained to the Board that I wanted the mural to make them feel as though they were there too—with the sun and the light and the trees and the wonderful, young, eager faces, bold and determined, looking toward their next assignment, engagement, the next encounter with the North. I received nods and smiles.

Calling me on the following morning, four-star General Ray Davis—a US Marine Corp Medal of Honor recipient and at that time the Co-Chair of the Memorial Foundation—said, "Resolute! You can call their expressions . . . Resolute."

The Medal of Honor was awarded to Lt Col Raymond G. Davis in 1952 for action in December 1950 when he was commanding office of the 1st Battalion, 1st Marine Division in Korea. The Citation starts. . . . *For conspicuous gallantry and intrepidity at the risk of his life above and beyond the call of duty as commanding officer of the 1st Battalion, in action against enemy aggressor forces.* Davis led his battalion to rescue an isolated and near defeated company during the nightmare withdrawal from the Chosin Reservoir disaster in Korea. Advancing in stealth for 8 miles off the mountain roads in radio-silence, and over 3 successive ridges deep in snow and the dead of a dark frozen winter night, he found the remaining soldiers of Company F and their Captain William Earl Barber near daybreak. Davis and his men relieved the beleaguered rifle company who was sure to receive another searing and endless firefight from the Communist Chinese, similar to the many firefights during the preceding weeks. He engaged in hand-to-hand encounters. In so doing, while leading his men, Davis seized and opened the vital Toktong Pass, freeing the only route available for two marine regiments in danger of being cut off by superior hostile forces during their re-deployment to the port of Hungnam, all while under savage fire from a determined "foe" while carrying all his wounded with him, including 22 litter cases and numerous ambulatory patients. The citation ends with. . . . *His valiant devotion to duty and unyielding fighting spirit in the face of almost insurmountable odds enhance and sustain the highest traditions of the US Naval Service.* *

"Resolute!" said Ray Davis. The whole mural would have a sense of steadfast and, yes, *resolute* service. Not only service to the troops as embodied in the three-dimensional sculptures that would be positioned in front of the wall, but also to the visitors, the people "back home," the citizens of the United States and the citizens of the world as they would be reflected in the mural wall.

Linda started sending me selections of photos, a broad range to see what I liked, most meeting my needs, others with faces turned to the side, some talking to their friends, some smiling, a few looking most serious. Over the next months we grew an army of suitable faces, portraits of Americans. Along the way, I decided I shouldn't know who these people were and asked Linda to keep their identities from me, maintain their anonymity, for they would be representing all those who served in Korea.

In the midst of this process, my father's life came rushing to me. Dad, who didn't finish high school, had a deep interest in radio and electronics. He worked very hard and before the war, educated himself at night in electrical engineering. While employed with a manufacturing firm on a government contract during the war, he designed the Navy's World War II shipboard portable megaphone and "loud hailer"—as he called it. I guess seeing a few photos of the Navy made the connection in my memory; the equipment my dad designed was undoubtedly used aboard ships off Korea. I assume he received a draft deferment during WWII because of his engineering skills. I never asked

---

* The full Citation by the Department of the Navy awarding Lt Colonel Raymond G. Davis is in the Supplement.

him or Mom about that. It never occurred to me. In those years before the war, he and his brother Karl were avid amateur photographers. Boxes of his black-and-white prints were carefully placed in our apartment's closets, top shelf, high up near the ceiling. After the war, he went on to design complex electronic wiring systems for aircraft, small jets and larger transport planes.

I thought there were so many ways to look at the wall and create the mural: up close to see the look in the eyes; from afar to see the overall patterns and the strength of the composition and its subtlety. Portraits were my dominant vision for the mural. Yet, there were so many ways of achieving that concept. Initially, I had thought the portraits would be large—ten feet high—so that the story of the war could easily be seen in their faces, told in the eyes, and grasped from afar. Literally. I wanted to achieve not only an understanding of the content of the individual portraits but to also give the viewer a changing experience. From a distance they could see images of large faces, looking out. As the viewer walked closer, those faces would seem to dissolve, become less recognizable because of the half-tone dot patterns by which they were made. Simultaneously, new smaller portraits or personal details, such as an engraving of a letter home, would emerge—all previously hidden in the same dot patterns. It seemed that both the size of the portraits and the graphic technique could be pretty interesting and work well.

However, the Commission of Fine Arts wished to shift the memorial's configuration. Further, I was told that J. Carter Brown, the commission's Chair, was nervous about having "super portraits" on the mall. I would now have to find solutions for the wall mural that would accommodate the Commission as well as the Advisory Board. Responding to Brown's concerns, I made the images smaller. Much smaller. Many portraits were reduced to life size, heads about a foot high so that the visitors would see the soldier's faces in equal size to their own. Their face reflected in the polished granite alongside those of the soldiers. They could look into the eyes of the men and women and have a silent conversation—just as you would with your friend. Other portraits would be smaller, assisting in creating a sense of distance and space on the long granite wall. Just faces. Only the men and women. I showed the Board my latest direction. General Richard G. Stilwell, chairman of the Veterans Advisory Board, liked the concept, agreed that there should be as little as possible added to define their occupation; "it need not be specific," he said. Later, he pulled me aside for a private chat. "Just enough to tell us of their job... their head gear or maybe something in their hands, a wrench. Nothing else." Stilwell said. "No tanks or jets." He made his thoughts public to the Board.

I suspect part of his response was to have the Korean War Veterans Memorial Mural wall decidedly different from the Vietnam Memorial across the Reflecting Pool. He never said this directly, however I could sense his silent thoughtful reasoning, particularly when earlier I mentioned the possibility and showed alternative ideas to portraits; letters, battle scenes, or just faces. Just head and shoulders. One clean simple idea.

At the onset of the project and before meeting General Stilwell, I read he had been with the Central Intelligence Agency. Somewhat concerned, I wanted to know more, to see with whom I was getting involved. Judy remembered he had been mentioned in Neil Sheehan's book about John Paul Vann and the Vietnam War, *A Bright Shining Lie*. I found the book on our shelves and re-read the parts about Stilwell's service in Vietnam. Stilwell had rebutted "the arguments of Vann" and others, who believed the US was losing the Vietnam War as early as 1963. Stilwell became Chief of Staff to General William Westmoreland, General Paul Harkins' successor, and "had gradually realized that he had been wrong about Vann and had come to admire him." At Vann's funeral in June 1972 at Arlington National Cemetery, Lt. General Stilwell, now the Army's deputy chief of staff for military operations, asked to be a pallbearer.

General Stilwell had a brilliant career in the Army, from graduating in the 1938 class at West Point, through Commander-in-Chief of the United Nations Command. In the early 1970s he was Commander-in-Chief of the United States Forces in Korea. He was with the CIA from 1949 until 1952, when he was posted as chief of the Far East Division, Central Intelligence Agency.

I looked forward to working with him and would grow to greatly respect his candor and judgment. His presence was decidedly evident when one entered the room. I assumed he was not an easy man to get close to. He had clear concise responses to a question I asked about his recent return from Korea and the demeanor of the people in the North. "What might you expect from a people in fear and not well fed?" he responded. In his serious determined, straight talking manner, General Stilwell had a special sense of listening. In private, the two of us would talk design concepts and strategic details—why the simple idea of portraits was important, and nothing should complicate the visual message of the mural. I write "talk." I did not write "discuss." He didn't seem to give room to explore ideas. He saw what he liked and stuck with it, pretty much spoke in dictums. After all, he was a "Four Star" and led this advisory group of retired field grade officers. I saw this as others delivered their presentations. However, he always honored what each individual said. He had a decisive grasp of design strategies in his talks with me, and with the sculptor, Frank Gaylord—and as I can only imagine, with the architects and the members of his Advisory Board as well.

The holidays were soon upon us and I decided to send a simple gift to the General and his wife, a vase designed by Frank Lloyd Wright. General Stilwell died suddenly on Christmas Day 1991, before the memorial design was finalized.

I attended a memorial service for him at Fort McNair. All the high-level dignitaries were present including General Colin Powell on down. I don't recall seeing anyone from the Memorial Advisory Board, nodded hello to a few officers I thought I recognized and found a seat. The service was simple, straightforward, a few remarks and it was over. I found my way back to National Airport and flew home. A few months later, I happened to have a conversation with the General's son, Dick Stilwell, a retired officer and by then an actor. He asked if I had sent his parents a Christmas gift. "Yes, I did." He thanked me on behalf of his mother. I would very much miss General Stilwell.

Not long after General Stilwell's death, Bob Hansen, the Executive Director of the Board came to me with a big smile on his face. Contrary to the General's explicit directions, Hansen said he and his colleagues decided they wanted the mural to include implements of war—tanks and artillery and jets, fighters and bombers. Shocked, I reminded him of General Stilwell's instructions to me and the Board. He just smiled again. I said I'd consider their thoughts. In the end, I was unable to hold back the tide, but thankfully I was successful in convincing the Board that the mural was to serve the veterans and not be a military recruiting poster on the national mall. The tanks and airplanes and trucks became secondary, faintly etched in the background—thereby General Stilwell's wish to highlight the faces was honored. I miss you, General.

꒰ℳ꒱

My office-studio was in Greenwich Village, in Manhattan, on the third floor of the old *Village Voice* building, at the corner of University Place and East

11th Street. Its 3,000 square-foot corner space, and glorious southern light, was perfect for dealing with the army of portraits. To facilitate the job, I devised a system of 4 x 8-foot movable pin-up boards that could easily be shifted around. As we received images from Linda, Jennifer would enlarge them in different sizes on the copy machine, and pin them up on the boards. We would study them, rearrange them in various patterns in order to get a sense how best they might look on the National Mall. Three walls of the studio and the spaces between the windows were covered with portraits, as were the walls in the conference room. We'd photograph slides of one wall and project them on another; some of these we used in my presentations to the Advisory Board and the architects in DC. It was just another way to facilitate composing a 164-foot-long mural. We'd integrate some of these arrangements into the graphic understructure, the basic concept of the mural and see how the mural flowed sideways, left to right, from one end to the other.

For the next three years my team and I worked on the final selection of two, nearly three thousand faces and their layout on the wall. We carefully considered every one of them, contemplated them, moved them around, edited them, re-composed them, refined them, retouched the lighting when needed so that, as planned, all their faces were evenly illuminated from the east by the morning sun—to give the impression that the entire composition of portraits had been taken at the same time, on the same day, in the same light, in Korea.

Initially, the composition was intuitive and to a certain degree, annoyingly arbitrary. I became uncomfortable with the unstructured nature of its appearance. As things happen, I remembered seeing a film by David Hockney and Philip Haas about a very special seventeenth century Chinese scroll (called "The Kangxi Emperor's Southern Inspection Tour (1691–1698), scroll seven.") at New York's Metropolitan Museum of Art. This film, A *Day on the Grand Canal with the Emperor of China*, became most important in composing a continuous canvas, to refresh the traditional signals for implying movement in and out of distance and not rely on aerial perspective. The mural of engraved granite would be 164 feet long and 12 feet tall at its highest end. I

FOLLOWING SPREAD: The Faces in the Korean War Veterans Memorial Mural

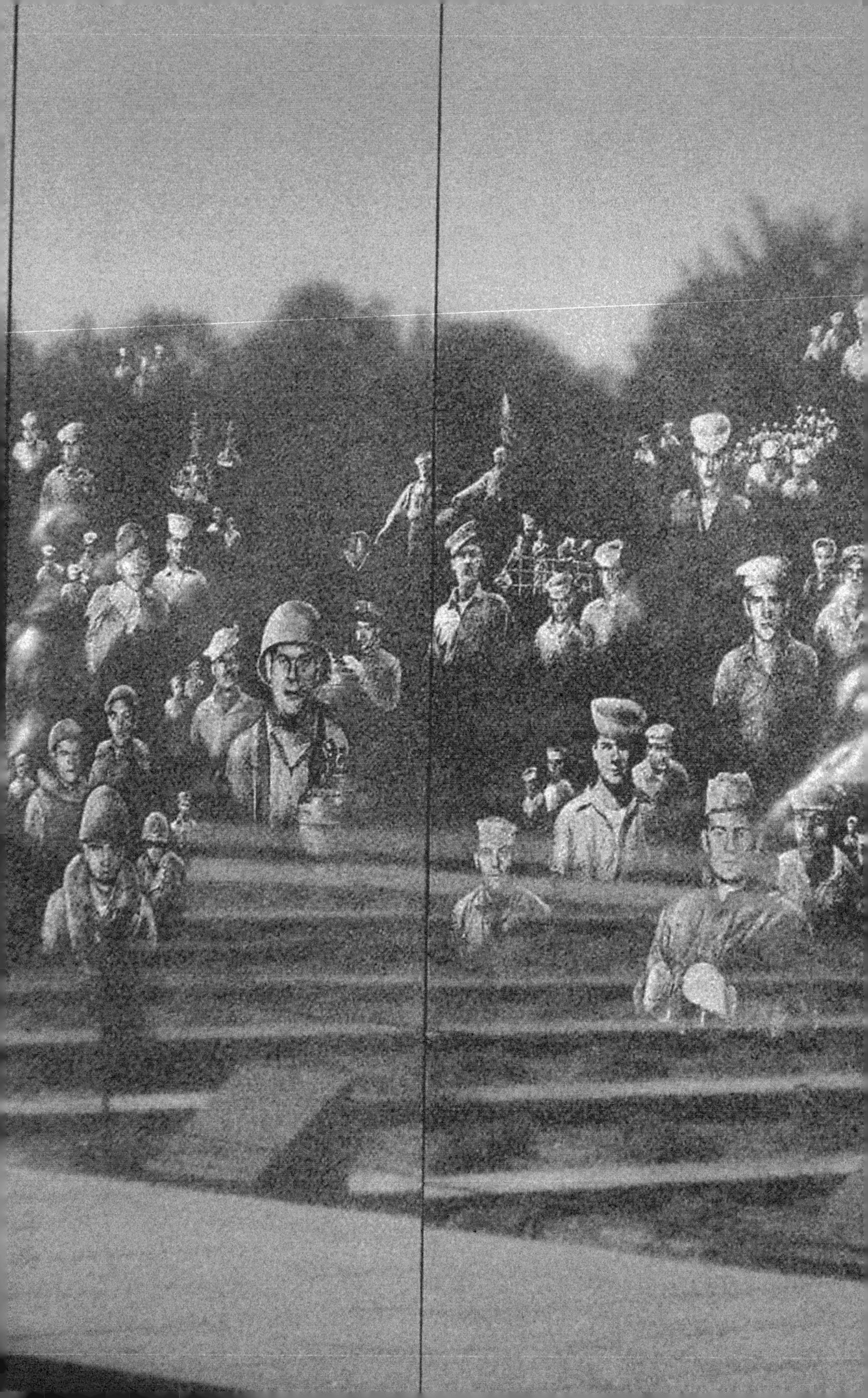

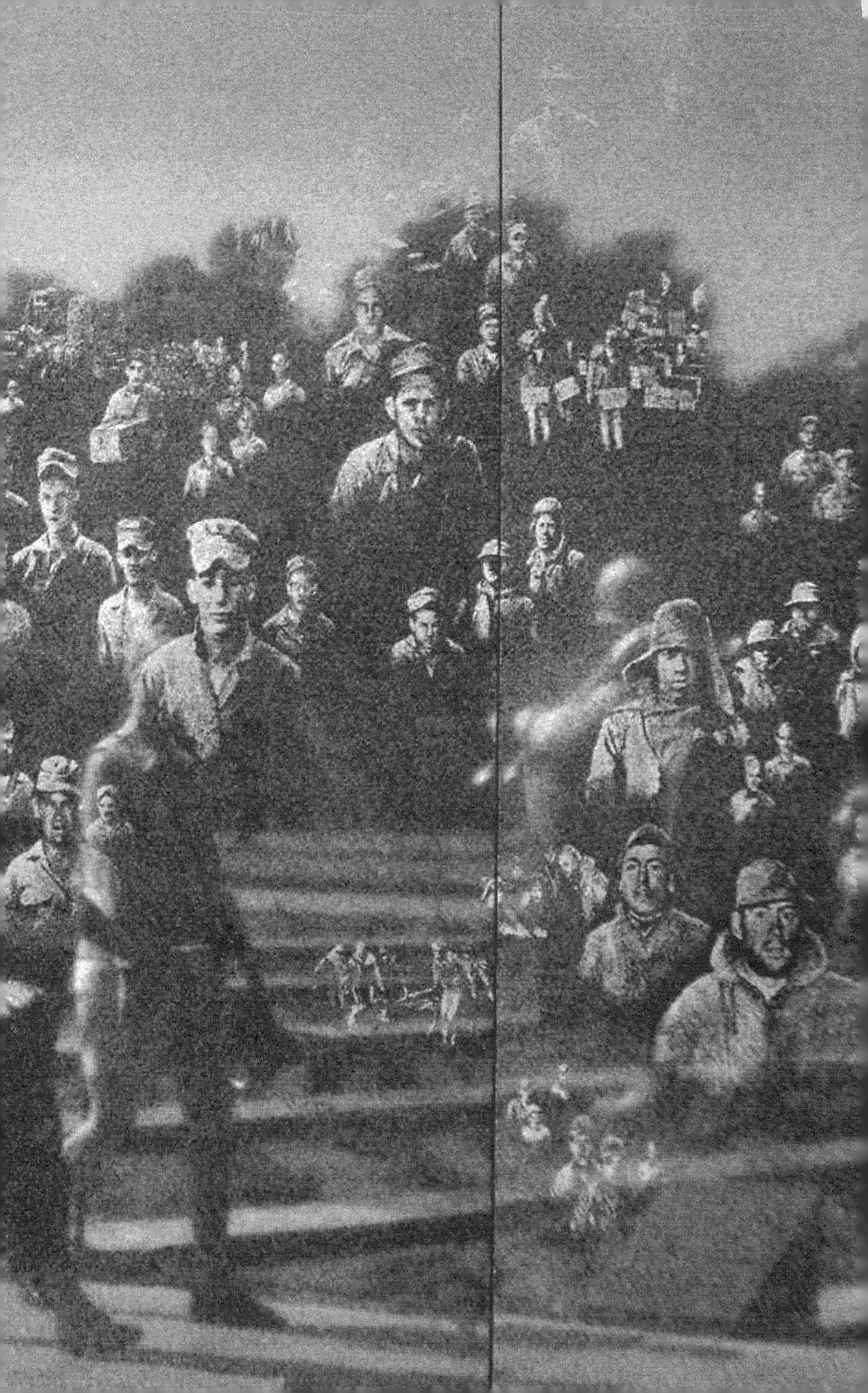

wanted to deal with this continuous granite "scroll" without using the traditional graphic signals of space. In my way of thinking, the wall was to maintain its own two-dimensional integrity and not lose its surface to imply depth and space. I had not yet fully realized the importance of another dimension—the reflective quality of the polished stone would add depth during the day. At night the mural became mystically surreal and ghost-like under low-level illumination. The wall disappeared and the portraits emerged floating in the dark space before you—an amazing gift from the grit-blasted images in the granite, the eyes and the portraits, the illumination. You meet the faces from the past and somehow, they appear together across time; otherworldly! Yet, very present.

I started developing a graphic understructure based on the geometry of the wall—diagonal axis lines ("force lines" was the term used by many) emanating from the corners of the four-foot-wide panels. With this change in height, from six feet to twelve feet, the angle of the diagonal line would slightly vary from one panel to another, creating its own movement. I liked this effect. With that, we could start to develop patterns and the composition would finally evolve into its own structured organization based on its inherent architecture.

I looked carefully at these geometric patterns. My team and I worked diligently to adjust that geometry and then tested it to see how it would function. We applied ovals or dots, simulating a face to test the placement of portraits. In this pattern—fondly dubbed "the constellation diagram" by Kent Cooper—every dot in the constellation represented a face. It gave me a master plan to design the memorial's panels. There was to be a sequence of different groups of occupations in each of the services—from truck drivers to pilots, from signal men on aircraft carriers to telephone operators in the field, tank commanders, boatswains, beach masters, bridge builders, doctors, nurses, cooks... the list includes all the work of the men and women who served in support of the fighting forces—thousands, all anonymous, all in Korea, all American.

The diagonal axis lines created the zones to organize placement of the faces within each group, their relationship with adjacent groups, the flow from an aesthetic point of view between the groups, and the flow of occupations. Over two thousand portraits. It took a long time, but we worked it out.

And from a distance, this understructure of lines, the constellation diagram and composition of portraits would merge to resemble the skyline of the mountains in Korea.

At one of the last reviews with the Fine Arts Commission, Carter Brown said the mural wall was highly imaginative and reminiscent of the photojournalism of the period; he made a remark about keeping tourists away from the statues at the Korean War Veterans Memorial in order to have purity in the sculptural landscape—to keep it clean and devoid of loud voices and loud shirts in multi-colored, flowered prints. At that time, I preferred the "Hawaiian Shirts" be able to wander within the aisles of juniper and be closer to these larger-than-life warriors. Today, I believe Brown was correct to keep Frank's sculptures together, reading as a whole . . . undisturbed.

As far as I can tell, my mural, this mural of portraits of men and women serving their country, taken by military photographers in Korea between 1950 and 1953, is the largest and most extensive photographic exhibition of people in the United States, and I'd be surprised if not the world.

Burghers of Calais

Come a day we'll honor all those who have died
And remember the less fortunate ones
Remember the less fortunate ones

FOUR
REMEMBER

The cab dropped me off at Daniel Chester French Drive, near the Lincoln Memorial where the tour buses stand idling. Every time I'm in Washington, I visit the Mall, pulled there to spend a moment with my old friends, see who else is visiting.

Over the years, I have identified five, perhaps six attributes of a memorial. A memorial *commemorates* an event. It *remembers* a time; *honors* a person. It builds on our own *understanding* and the meaning of what happened. At best, it places that understanding in broader personal, global terms. With that understanding, it engages the viewer's imagination, for without the viewer there is no memorial. It brightens an inner meaning, held in the heart as it touches our soul. All that being said, hopefully it *inspires* us to step beyond our imagination toward a refreshed vision of our tomorrow. And, in that process, a memorial *heals*. It is a marker for places to remember, for it is in places that we must go to gather and remember. To tell stories. And search for answers.

The search has taken time and the path seems to have wound around in ways I couldn't have planned. I've come across many detours in the road; gone down paths that led me to helping others, to giving talks for close friends newly departed; down a wholly different path, one filled with unmitigated sorrow.

I've become most fond of a particular sculpture, a grouping of bedraggled men who had come together hundreds of years ago to face their future. It happened in another country. Yet, this sculpture is akin in sensibility to the sculptures in the Korean Memorial and the Lincoln Memorial. The story it tells, like the other two, is haunting. In 1347, during The Hundred Years War, the English King Edward III, after winning battles in surrounding France, captured and held the town of Calais hostage for nearly a year. King Philip of France enticed Calais's citizens to hold out at all costs. The town suffered the siege while starvation and desperation mounted. A group of six, the burghers, the elite of the town offered themselves as prisoners if Edward would lift the siege and let all other citizens go free. The six knew they would be killed in return for their surrender.* The English Queen consort, Philippa of Hainault, was serving as regent during the king's absence from his conquest across the Channel. Learning of the brave actions of the six to save their fellow citizens, Philippa intervened to save their lives, claiming that their death would be a bad omen to the birth of Edward's and her soon to be born child. This act of kindness would help maintain peace throughout the British realm during King Edward III's fifty-year reign.

In 1880, the people of Calais decided they wanted a memorial to honor the burghers. After he went to Calais to help find the perfect place for the monument, Auguste Rodin accepted the commission for the sculpture. The renowned artist started work on *The Burghers of Calais* in 1884. Eleven years later, in 1895, the first in a series of casts was placed in a prominent city park in Calais.

The casting I often see at New York's Metropolitan Museum of Art is powerful, set in the light of the windows facing Central Park—light that pours over the gnarled, twisted, powerful bodies of these brave men. The burgher's hands are enormous, reaching to grasp salvation. The group is tightly compact, dragging chains and wearing nooses of entrapment and defeat in self-sacrifice after the English yearlong siege. Just as we recognize the power of Lincoln or the soldiers in the Korean Memorial, we see the valor of these captives. We may not know what happened in 1347, but we understand their despair, simply by seeing this work of art. Rodin's sculpture was unique at the

---

*Other historic writing contends Edward demanded the six appear with nooses around their necks. Still other variations to the story discuss the tradition of the time; details in the Chronicles of Jean Froissart (c1333-c1400) and the chronicler Jean Le Bel (c1290-c1370).

time, when most monuments were heroic and showed victory. Here was a symbol of an epic story of the defeat of a town and a battle, honoring the six who were ready to give their lives to save the slaughter of the citizens.

Between 1900 and 1949, six marches on the National Mall occurred (eight marches are shown on another list) including 5,000 who marched in 1913 in support of *Women's Suffrage;* 50,000 who marched in 1925 in favor of the Klu Klux Klan! Most Extraordinary! The Klu Klux Klan! How could that have happened? I'm disgusted to find this, a march in my nation's capital honoring a racist group we knew supported black lynching in many states. How times have changed, yet have they? In 1932, 20,000 WWI vets gathered in tents during the height of the Great Depression, seeking advanced payment of a promised bonus from the Hoover Administration. Two vets were killed. General Douglas MacArthur squelched their protest—the bonus was never paid by the Hoover Administration; however it was paid by the FDR administration.

The first recorded march on the National Mall was by Coxey's Army, a protest march by unemployed American workers in 1894. The Mall was in grave need of rehabilitation at this time. Repairs would start in 1902. But its condition in 1894 didn't deter Coxey's Army. The march was led by Jacob Coxey, an Ohio businessman, during the second year of a four-year depression caused by the Panic of 1893, the worst in America's history to that day. Its purpose was to lobby the government to create jobs by building roads and other public works. The march originated with one hundred men in Ohio, eventually numbering six thousand who camped on a farm site in nearby Maryland. The leaders were arrested for walking on the grass of the Capitol. Participating was L. Frank Baum who wrote *The Wonderful Wizard of Oz*, the mythic tale of the adventures of Dorothy, a scarecrow, a lion and a tin man along a yellow brick road, all symbolizing, it is thought, the time, the march and passion of Coxey's Army in 1894.

The number of events dramatically increased in subsequent decades. During the Vietnam War there were many anti-war marches—I was there, Judy was there for a few, and you and many of your friends probably were, too. Between 1970 and 1999 there were over forty gatherings: the Gulf War

National Victory Celebration on June 8, 1991 (although not a protest, you'll see in a future chapter its dramatic effect on the Korean War Veterans Memorial), the Rally for Women's Lives in 1994 and the Million Man March in 1995, among them. Between 2000 and 2009, there were thirty-nine marches including three marched who opposed the Iraq War in 2007. The American public grew in their solidarity for a purpose. That's not unusual for this Mall—nor for any national event where people gather to honor, commemorate, perhaps inspire. *And heal.*

On a July afternoon in 2015, I flew to Washington to review the site for a newly proposed National World War I Memorial in Pershing Park, adjacent to the Willard Hotel, a block or so from the White House. It's a curious space, already occupied by a memorial to General Pershing on one side and the remnants of an ice-skating rink on the other. From there, I walked over to the National Mall. The gravel pathway crunched beneath my feet as a cooling breeze softened the summer heat. Other visitors came from all cultures and many places to see the Korean and the Vietnam War Veterans Memorials, to visit the Washington Monument and the Lincoln Memorial, the World War II Memorial. Visitors from Vietnam and Korea, Japan, Russia, England and Germany. From Ohio, California, New York, Florida, New Hampshire, Montana and Colorado. Young and old. Rappers, rockers and long hairs. Classes from Bethesda and students from Denver. Families from Salt Lake City and Seattle. I looked at them. They looked at the memorials. It was all the same as before, except the people. Yet, they were the same, identical in their individuality. Maybe there were more school groups this time.

When people visit a memorial, I sense that they change—almost imperceptibly. Teenagers stand slightly straighter, some giggle, perhaps quietly, feeling uncomfortable in the formality of Lincoln or Jefferson. Some looking very comfortable sit on the steps, older couples seem serious, casting respect in their own way. A man softly hums to himself. Younger couples walking, some hand in hand, one or two with strollers, most side-by-side, each lost in meditative silence. There's an ease about them. Calmness and infinite respect. Politeness. Some groups you might otherwise think will be rowdy are transformed. A hush covers the many sitting on the steps of the Lincoln

Monument; a stillness likened to the quiet at Union Square the evening of 9/11 in New York. Something is happening in that silence. They walk to the memorial of World War II, passing Vietnam on one side and Korea to the south. Others saunter by the nearly hidden marble gazebo of the District of Columbia World War I memorial. They look and read. In some places, tears are shed. They think. They talk with one another. I don't hear them. They're making sounds, listening in conversation. I don't know what they're saying. The power of this place brings serenity to my soul, silence to my inner senses. I don't hear the child crying. I don't hear the tour buses idling near Lincoln. Nor the jets taking off from National Airport. Nor the helicopters flying overhead. Those sounds belong in another place.

Places and objects on the Mall are designed in the vision of those who brought them to life, those who willed their use... and for those who come to visit them... to rally support for a cause in the spirit of what the memorials represent; and for those who share their spirit and the need to remember. A veteran. A father. A sweetheart. A friend from a distant country. Or even for someone you don't know. A gathering of many to support freedom. In that process, a memorial unfolds its true meaning. Yes, a good memorial should help us heal—heal as an individual and as a nation. It happens over and over with the Vietnam Veterans Memorial.

In looking at a memorial, rarely do I understand the "how" in its details. Seldom do I bring my mind to understand the details of what I see. They're here. And I accept what is here. Mostly I sense what has been missing inside of me, or I feel closure in answer to a vague question. What is important at each memorial, is the chance I have to change my tomorrow, not just look over my shoulder toward another time passed for a departed companion but look forward to a new understanding and a new future for me, for my family, for us. Some of these people may feel likewise. Others may have other needs... perhaps to advocate Civil Rights, Women's Rights or to see the AIDS Quilt. Or to protest a disservice. I can go beyond taking things for granted. I can raise questions. What I see is a deep hidden understanding that has surfaced here on the Mall at this time.

Here is the national place to celebrate America, established during a dinner meeting between Thomas Jefferson, Alexander Hamilton and James Madison in New York City in 1790, managed by George Washington and designed by his colleague Pierre Charles L'Enfant.

I grew up learning and loving abstract relationships in painting and sculpture and design—Helen Frankenthaler, David Smith, Barnett Newman, Alexander Calder, Dale Chihuly, Charles Eames, Eero Saarinen. Georgia O'Keeffe. Over the years, I became aware of my smile and the joy I felt going through art museums and walking along city blocks here and in Europe, listening to statesmen as well as to people on the street talk of the human needs, I became more attracted to figurative works, such as those of Rodin, Monet and Turner. Matisse and Vuillard. Brâncuși. They have meaning to me as I can see the human condition in them.

I had been helping several commissions in downtown New York City after the 9/11 terrorist attacks. I chaired discussions with families of the victims regarding their needs for a memorial. I found the families' needs were generally similar, uniform in wanting to recognize their loved ones. They held fast to principles of remembrance and honor. However not all the lives lost on 9/11 were American. There were people from ninety-six different countries and nationalities killed or injured in the World Trade Center attack. Picking up on that statistic at one family session, to see the nature of grief, I proposed a new Center for Conflict Resolution as a platform for a memorial of 9/11. A place where groups and government could meet and discuss. A father said that would be a good productive solution. Others picked up on the theme. Although later I formally proposed the concept to a member of the City Council, it never gained traction. It might have been too raw and too soon after the event.

Unlike Rodin's Burghers in near black bronze, positioned close together, Frank Gaylord's Korean War soldiers in bright stainless steel are spaced apart, alert in their anticipation of an impending shot, protected from the elements in their ponchos, realistic in their pursuit of cause—two compositions, so different yet close to each other. Six dark Burghers, heads down-cast, distorted features and posture, all closely knit in one unit expressing despair in losing a year-long effort as well as the probability of their own lives. Nineteen bright energetic, alert soldiers spaced far apart, yet in tight visual contact, a formation of unity, ready for any challenge or impediment they may encounter. Black and white. Close and distant. Rodin's and Gaylord's two sculptural arrangements stand across time in different countries, dissimilar in stance, story and anticipated outcome, yet both evoking a strong emotional feeling in the observer... hope and strength intermixed with pity and helplessness. We instantly see each and immediately know their story.

What do we know of the persons represented by the traditional sculptures in parks that we walk by? Of the Civil War generals on horseback, what do they stand for? By convention the position of a steed's hoofs told of his rider's fate. One hoof in the air means the rider died of wounds suffered in battle; two means the rider was killed on the battlefield. Four hoofs on the ground means the rider died a natural death. At Gettysburg, Longstreet's mount clearly has one hoof raised; yet he did not die at Gettysburg, nor in any other battle, but long after while serving in Washington's diplomatic service; of pneumonia, a natural death. (Rules are broken, and explanation might not even be made). The exception must sometimes prove the rule.

What do we know of Horace Greeley, William Cullen Bryant or Isidor Straus? Of the three, Straus we may know the least. He was a co-owner of Macy's Department Store, who together with his wife, Ida, drowned on April 15, 1912, in the sinking of the *Titanic* (she not wanting to be separated from him). A memorial to them rests as a reclining figure at a quiet pool of water in a mini park at Broadway and 106th Street, near their residence in New York City. It is not a sculpture of the couple. Yet as we look at it, we look backward in time. We consider our thoughts to make a similar decision about life. What makes us want to know their history and why they are here? Details are rarely given on a plaque next to a sculpture—unless it is in a museum. Yet, there is seldom a need. The story is usually told by the sculptor in the shape, stance and countenance of his or her work. There, it is heard in the heart of the observer.

Here are the differences between public and private memorials. They both serve the same purpose. Private memorials have intimate, very personal meanings. A mother gone too soon. A son lost in a snowstorm. Public memorials carry the broader tasks of conveying the significance of an event for a group of people, a mass of people; creating a place to remember, honor, commemorate and hopefully, heal; bringing meaning to each of the many visitors to make this time at the memorial matter ... and clocks this in a sense of alluring beauty to exist in tomorrow's time. Still, even within a large group, each experience becomes very personal, remembering a buddy lost in a war, or a liberty restored as with the service of an admired individual, be it Abraham Lincoln, Thomas Jefferson or Franklin Delano Roosevelt, Martin Luther King, Jr. ... or the visitor's squad leader when he served in the Army.

In the end, we are given a chance to heal. A chance to take the time. Healing is a mysterious process of life. Grieving is a step toward healing. We mourn, draped in black; in other cultures, in white or red. Some howl in grief. Others sing, dance and laugh. Wakes. Sitting shiva. Memorial services. Later, we have a stone, or a plaque added to the burial site—something to mark the place and the person and the time; we call this headstone a memorial, perhaps a monument. Others build a crypt, with their family name on the building, a door opening into a space for private meditation. Afterward, we walk away—at times, we return, flowers in hand to lay on the grave or in the mausoleum, as a means to remember; others leave a memento, a photograph. Perhaps, this is our way of not fully letting go. Time seems to float. Some of us look to identify with others in our grief.

Seemingly, events after a loss happen in measures of time, traditional in most cultures. A week. A month. A year. Yet, as a culture we tend to rush to do *something*, to take *some* action, *now*. Such was the case with the memorial surrounding the September 11th attacks at New York's World Trade Center, the Pentagon in Washington, DC and near Shanksville, Pennsylvania. This is certainly needed at times in our life. Another place, deep within us, urges patience and the passage of time.

At the age of thirty-three, my stepson, Judy's son, Clark, took his life in 1992. Judy and I dealt with the tragic loss both together and separately. Judy initially cancelled all her concerts; however, after talking to Joan Rivers, who told her not to quit, that she needed to honor Clark and to do so by living her life. Judy went back on the road. I went with her for a couple weeks, her mother and sister joining her in the mountain towns by rushing rivers, and the wide-open endless spaces in Arizona and Colorado, healing spaces to grieve and to laugh and to sing. But I also wished to be alone and bury myself in solitude and my projects. I took walks and veered off to visit places that made me comfortable. Although I was in the midst of designing a national memorial, I realized I had to seek help, at least I learned to seek help—from my family, from a friend—a respected counsel—from a professional. I looked to a volume of meditations or the books of our religion, glanced through many of them, probably read some or most of them. Judy and I talked with our friend, Jim Morton, Dean at the Cathedral of St. John the Divine; he was most helpful and suggested we keep Clark in our vision and thoughts....and not question too much.

In the early raw months after Clark's death, Iris Bolton, a new friend of Judy's, whose son had also taken his life, sent Judy her book about the suicide, *My Son . . . My Son . . . .* Iris ran a center for mental health in Atlanta, called *The Link*. Her husband, Jack, told me, "They'll all ask you how she's doing, never ask you how you're doing." Iris said there would eventually be an equivalent benefit from this tragedy—some gift to me from Clark. I wasn't able to understand this. I heard what she was saying, but I couldn't comprehend it, couldn't make it fit. Yet, following this tragedy, Clark's daughter, Hollis, my step-granddaughter, began to spend more and more time with us in New York. Not having children of my own, I was given this extraordinary time with her as a gift: watching her grow; giving a talk to her class in New York about the memorial I was designing in Washington—all arranged by Holly who wanted to show off her papa; and listen to her questions. Judy and I always told Hollis the truth about her father's death, and when she was in school in New York at Marymount, in first grade, she came home one day and said, "I told them all about my life and all about daddy's death. I wanted them to know what really happened. I didn't want them to make something up." She loved photographs of the wall that I was designing and wanted to know about Korea and this design—and life. Why her father was gone, why this memorial was to be built and where, all mixed together and making sense in her thinking.

In time, Judy and I felt some form of permanent remembrance was needed for her son Clark, and some method of helping, of reaching out to others. We started a foundation and looked for ways to deal with suicide. Soon, we decided to mark Clark's loss with a memorial. We hunted to give shape to a memorial in keeping with Clark's spirit. It seemed it should be placed on the banks of the Mississippi in St. Paul, Minnesota in the park by the river, where he always walked, where he would take us when we visited—where his ashes were scattered. We decided on a bench. I gave it a design, and my friends at

Coldspring Granite (who were building the Korean Veterans mural) built it for Judy and me; Judy composed the inscription:

> *Beloved Son, Husband, Father, Nephew, Cousin, Friend.*
> *Clark Collin Taylor*
> *January 1959–January 1992*
> *Deeply Mourned–Free at Last*

Designing the memorial and working through that process helped me to turn grief toward joy by reaching out rather than stuffing my feelings of loss and anger into a receptacle of forgetfulness. We were able to start the process, bring a design into a form and finally let go of the countless details, then trust others to bring it into reality. Clark's bench was eventually installed at the edge of a lake on the grounds at Hazelden in Center City, Minnesota, the mother of recovery and treatment centers for substance abuse. Clark had achieved sobriety at Hazelden seven years before his death, where a young man or woman in the throes of getting sober might rest awhile, lie back, rest their head against the granite pillow, gaze out across that lake, perhaps get in touch with that new peace of sobriety and find some solace and comfort.

The essence of a memorial is as time passes; the person's sense of remembrance enhances understanding opening pathway to healing. And hope.

Public monuments take on many forms: a statue, a wall, even a sphinx. They may be structures extraordinarily large in scale, such as the pyramids in Egypt, grand and noble, each honoring a Pharaoh resting therein along with his treasures. The form may also be noticeably humble, as is the statue of *Gandhi*, tucked away in Manhattan's Union Square, far away from his homeland in India, forever walking northward in a garden of flowers and greenery; or self-effacing, as is the one of *Eleanor Roosevelt* with a smile on her lips, in Riverside Park, leaning back amid the trees and gazing eastward—it is the only sculpture of a modern woman in the New York City park system. Other women include *Joan of Arc* in Riverside Park and the fictional *Alice* in her Central Park Wonderland.

They may be single and isolated in space as is Admiral Nelson atop the column in Trafalgar Square, London, or George Washington atop the pillar in Mount Vernon Place, Baltimore. Or more complex, like the Canadian National Memorial at Vimy, France. Memorials may also be a lonely plain, the site of an important event, unadorned and unmarked as might be said of the impossibly open, rising plain on which General Pickett's men charged the Union at Gettysburg, marked only in history's memory and statues at its edges to commemorate those who witnessed the bloodbath.

Here, standing on the Mall, I can now understand the "how" in the details of the memorial after contemplating them all, one by one as so many visitors do: the War Memorials; Korean War Veterans Memorial, Vietnam Veterans Memorial, World War I and World War II Memorials; and the Leaders Memorials; Washington Monument, Lincoln Memorial, Jefferson Memorial, Roosevelt Memorial and the Martin Luther King Jr. Memorials. Here, I can bring my mind to understand what I see. Mostly one senses what has been missing inside and now feeling closure gaining the answer to a vague question. At each memorial, I have a chance to change my tomorrow, look forward to a new understanding and a new future for me, for us. Here, I can go beyond taking things for granted. Here, I can raise questions. I can question what I see, what I know in my heart—disclosing a deep hidden understanding that has surfaced here at this memorial, at this moment. It comes with the time that I take to spend here, with myself.

My senses respond to what surrounds me. Seeing, hearing, touching, listening, smelling, and feeling in ways that I have not been aware.

Tall and wide. Flat or curved. Small yet delicate. Words, Music. Sound, Colors. Texture. Aroma. Separate and together, each memorial delights my eye and all my senses—whether I am aware of it or not. Each one gives substance to my memory. An obelisk. A phrase. Four musical notes. A smile. A name is mentioned, and I think of a person or place. Say the word "Korea" and the bitter cold winters of 1951 are instantly recalled for many; or a modern nation, thriving and prosperous. "Normandy," the blood-soaked beaches of D-Day and the rush to find shelter from the bullets; or the canvases of the

Impressionists. "Vietnam" points to hot, humid closeness of the jungle, the unforgivable decisions to keep sending our youth into the inferno; or to a million shades of green and fertile rice fields and smiles of the children. A long list of engraved names with mementos left behind at the base of two long triangular black, black walls.

The very nature of the memorial, its materials, and its structure contribute to the sound of each monument, enhancing the experience of it—whether it is the echo of hushed voices or the footfall on the stone in the shrine to Lincoln, around the Kennedy Eternal Flame in the Arlington National Cemetery, or the rush of falling water at the FDR memorial on the National Mall. In the background, the sound of the sea or the sound of the city or the muffled sounds of the people become an intrinsic part of the memorial too. And its aroma as I inhale the freezing cold of a winter's snow or breathe the humid heat of a July afternoon's dedication.

In a conversation over a quiet dinner, a friend asked me why no one seems to notice the statue of Daniel Webster in Central Park in New York City, while only a few feet away, crowds are ever present at the *Imagine* mosaic in the Strawberry Fields, the memorial to John Lennon. "Surely, we wouldn't be here were it not for Webster," my friend said with a knowing look.

I'm sure he understood why, for he is forever the learned journalist. My answer lies with the immediacy of time and the empathy that youth holds for the peace and respect of John Lennon and his music. Music draws, replenishes, inspires. It is dominant and surrounds us almost continuously. Ever-present. By contrast, I would imagine Daniel Webster's name is remotely familiar for some, yet unknown as to why a statue should bear that name.

Daniel Webster was a United States Senator, and in the late 1820s, during his first term, there was a southern bloc in Congress building against the influence of the financial and industrial power of the northern states. With America's expansion to the west, the South was pressing for the western states to join with them, the "slave states." Even the word *secession* was used. In January 1830, Robert Hayne, a southerner, suggested that a state may decide not to abide by a federal law if it wished to, thereby shredding the Union. There was a general feeling that the South had won this argument. Two days later,

Webster, the Massachusetts Senator, rose from the Senate floor to answer. A striking individual with a clarion voice and a deep look in his eyes, "Black Dan"—as he was called—addressed this pressing matter as to whether a state can so mitigate a Constitutional matter. One by one, he addressed Hayne's arguments. "It is, Sir, the people's Constitution, the people's government, made for the people, made by the people, and answerable to the people." Webster went on to explain, it was not the states prerogative to determine this matter. In a stirring soliloquy, eventually bringing much of the Senate and the gallery to tears, he looked to the strength of the Union, symbolized in our national flag of stars and stripes, ending his talk with, "Liberty and Union, now and forever, one and inseparable!" Webster saved the Union. For the time being. The argument, in various iterations of compromise under states' rights and slavery, would prevail in the Senate among Webster, John C. Calhoun and Henry Clay—the latter two, at that time, pro-slavery—and after their deaths, continue among other Senate members until 1861, when a compromise was no longer viable.

In today's youthful culture, I tell my dinner companion, Webster is of another generation, his long-ago words unable to compete for attention with Lennon and McCartney's streaming music—not to mention that Lennon's tragic murder happened only footsteps away from Daniel Webster's statue.

I believe the design of the two memorials shows that the reason for Webster's contemporary unpopularity may lie elsewhere; not time and music but one related to space.

Their physical sites, when compared with each other, are very different; simply put, one is not as compelling as the other. The space surrounding Daniel Webster's statue offers little room to congregate. Nearby vehicle traffic lanes run parallel with a pedestrian walkway almost under Webster's nose. It encourages one to move quickly past Mr. Webster. Meanwhile *Imagine* is in a tree-sheltered enclave with benches to rest and meditate and sing. *Imagine a world of no war—a planet of peace!* Webster is of the time of a "man on a horse" and *Imagine* is of today's era of landscape design and music. Time, space, and confusion of purposes all mix together in these two places, each serving different masters—obscuring the memory of Daniel Webster and the understanding of his story. There is no apparent living metaphor that pulls us to Mr. Webster, other than a national figure who delivered an eloquent objection to a call to abandon the US Constitution.

⌒❦⌒

The basis of all my work is the purity and simplicity of design relationships working hand in hand with the story, the clear narrative to move people to understand and perhaps take an action and assure their comfort in that process. At its core is that it must *matter*. This understanding has come through years of study—reading books on all subjects, fiction and non-fiction, histories, biographies, politics and mysteries; talking to people of many cultures and seeing how they live, work and play; listening to the songs and music that surround me; and tasting and touching places and objects as I've traveled. This extraordinary foundation has let me design those color skis that sing to the heart and change the picture of skiing in the world, packaging that whets the appetite, symbols that engender value, films that smooth the flickers in the mind, and information systems that help people find their way in the hustle of crowded airports, subways and web sites. The narrative is integral within the form. The form becomes the principal idea carrying the drama to the hearts and minds of my public. And the understanding of what brings meaning to the public in a National Memorial on the National Mall. It must matter.

⌒❦⌒

Designers hold a long tradition with space and materials, each possessed with meaning originating and deepening centuries ago. Each selected with reason. Chosen carefully, the materials enliven the form, touch our senses, and trigger our memory. The materials do not always meet an engineer's cost-benefit analysis (value-engineered as is the term these days), but more importantly they can instill a sense of humanity and emotional satisfaction. And Truth. When successful, the combination of materials and form pulls us to a fresh place, paving a new path.

The ancients looked to nature and its abundant variety of texture for the structure of their environments to bring meaning to their surroundings, supporting their lives. Their basic elements of all matter were the enduring— *EARTH, AIR, WATER, FIRE*. Before humanity knew the atomic structure of elements, early designers and philosophers hundreds of years before, saw life and growth entwined with their environment in all its magnificence. The materials and forms may be taken for granted, yet the metaphors are clear today, as they were to the Ancients—the Phoenicians, Chinese, Greeks and Romans—before the Norse and Portuguese set sail.

Earth. This is where we stand, our footing. It grounds us. It nourishes us with its bounty, allowing vegetation to grow in marvelous and diverse forms, while giving shelter and food. From the earth we quarry granite and marble, mine copper, gold and silver. Extract ore to make steel and bronze and glass to build our cities and bridges and the sculptures we encounter.

Air. It gives us life in our first breath; ends life when we exhale our last. It carries us. It lets us fly...and our souls soar. Air connects us to distant places. It is ever-present. It touches us in all ways. We cannot touch it, still we can feel it. Air brings aromas that trigger our memories and pleases us or warns us, recreating moments forgotten and giving us encouraging cues needed to take the next step, to face into its force. Air carries our meditative silence.

Water. The human body is composed mostly of water. It is the basic substance that surrounds us in our mother's womb. It is from the sea that life emerged and crawled up onto the shore. In circa 1488, Sandro Botticelli painted *The Birth of Venus,* the goddess coming forth, full born, from the oceans, standing within a shell. Water eases our communications and movement, as it does for the whales. It is a conduit. It refreshes us for the day. Without water, we have no life. Water binds the soil under our feet into earth. Not too much, nor too little.

Fire. The undying spirit of a person is embodied in the passion of fire—its ability to kindle, melt a new spirit and rebirth, as in the story of the Phoenix. Fire symbolizes the undying spirit of life, whether in an Olympic flame or the perpetual flame flickering at the gravesite of John F. Kennedy Memorial in Arlington National Cemetery.

As a designer I honor these ancient elements, as fresh today as long ago, to combine and give form, connect me and ground much of my understanding. They have become part of my memory. They support me. They are archetypes, the ethics of nature, the foundation on which my life is built and lived.

Aristotle identified the fifth element, *Aether* or *Ether*—a spiritual force related to celestial bodies, transmitting light within the realm of metaphysics. Best for me to honor the ancient philosopher and retain his number 5 as I move into a contemporary era of Time and Space. I understand and use these terms... together with many of my fellow designers.

Time. This is a sixth element. It is not the fleeting minutes of a day, but the enduring time of a material, an age. The material in a memorial is chosen to withstand time as well as its structural capabilities. Bronze and stainless steel are selected for certain sculptural applications, granite for others. Granite lives for centuries and is of the earth itself. It fits. Copper tarnishes. Iron and steel rusts, unless it is specially compounded. Gold is ageless, soft and malleable. Time is within each of the elements. It provides the sustenance for each, separately or in combination. It colors each state. Time is also the vehicle for transformation. We use time. We spend time.

Space, a seventh element. Each element, by inclusion or by omission, plays its part in a memorial. Yet the object is not complete without the space surrounding it and within it.

Space is different from air. It is the "sense" of space surrounding ourselves and it is the space we occupy. And the space occupied by others, objects, sculptures and buildings, living rooms and theaters and stages. All so easily taken for granted. Negative space is a negative form. It has shape and helps define the positive, physical form of the things we easily see. It is within space that we reside, move and think. It is the space between the soldiers in the Korean War Veterans Memorial, and the movement of that space through and around each soldier and his poncho that pulls them together into a unified whole. Herein is the totality of the design, the heart of the design—the relationship of positive and negative form supporting the idea and content of the memorial—the vision of the designer and the heartbeat of those who will come.

Color requires its own special note. Earth and fire have an emotional context . . . and descriptions as we may express them—brown and red. These colors are abundant in nature, as we all know. Earth provides minerals that make steel and bronze and stone. Their colors are inherently gray or black, or perhaps a full spectrum in variegated swirls and patterns, and reds, purples and yellows as we find in polished marbles, sulfur, or emeralds. Another predominant color in nature is the green in foliage or in some instances the bleached color of sand. Natural colors. And neutral colors. There is water . . . blue we might say, but really that's the reflection of the sky, yet on a cloudy day, water is dark blue or blue-black or, perhaps, grays.

The color of war might be represented by the green of the forest or the red of blood—complementary colors—opposites on the color wheel Yet, when mixed together they result in a value of gray—somberness, an appropriate tone for a memorial subject. White of Lincoln's marble sculpture is certainly more uplifting than the dark bronze of Jefferson. At least for me. White is the absence of color, or the presence of all the colors (in the terms of light physics). The faces on the Korean War Veterans Mural, etched in granite are near white and glow at night under indirect incandescent illumination. We are naturally drawn to light and brightness, to the future and hope.

The story chooses its color and materials. I simply help. A form responds to the narrative. It is the mournful black granite wall of the Vietnam War memorial, split to form two sharp pointed triangular walls that give substance to support the names. It is the long dark gray granite mural of the Korean War Veterans Memorial, etched with portraits that recall the newspaper photos and black and white television film of the era; it is that memorial's stainless statues glistening in the bright sun that contrasts to the reflective dark grey mural wall and coordinates with its white etched faces. It is the white marble of Lincoln that shines hope, the brilliance of his spirit. These materials are woven together to tell the essence of the story and the person.

The process of creation is enjoyment—oh! At times agony in getting to the bliss, the connected back-and-forth thinking and the relation between seemingly disassociated and unrelated thoughts of today and those still to come; fully knowing that the solution is just a moment away or around the corner. Frustrating, when I'm not satisfied with the results. However, it is solved as I stay in the process. Isn't that how life is? It is conditioned by the almost arbitrary route, or perhaps it is a defined route, presented by the surprises of each day: turning a corner, a friend's call, a chance encounter, another's view of an event at a party and how different or similar it is to mine; and living through a tragic event and its memory.

The basics. Today, the basics fill my time—the clarity of the story and fulfilling the human need. Lines, planes, and volumes filled my formal design education. Lessons and exercises in three and two-dimensional forms: static and dynamic shapes; curvilinear and rectilinear volumes; dominant, subdominant and subordinate relationships, all in abstract forms. The lessons started in 1954 when I entered Pratt Institute, a year after the Korean War ceased fire. When put together with purpose and reason, they make up the products and places of our lives—chairs, computers, phones, cars, seating in trains and planes, buildings and lobbies, museums, monuments and memorials, branding and most everything we see around us. It matters. It all matters. The smallest become grand.

I learned from these lessons by making small three-dimensional wire structures composed of three curves in space, then three different rectilinear plinths, followed by three totally different forms—a sphere, triangle and rectangular plinth—and eventually worked toward creating a "concavity" or "convexity" that you could say starts to resemble an Arp sculpture (only better), the relationship between positive and negative forms and the curves of a life. They were beautiful maquettes. I started to understand the principles. But frequently I was puzzled and didn't quite know what I was doing. Others in my class at Pratt Institute were as well. Always changing parts of the composition to satisfy the teacher. It was never right. Always needing improvement. Did I understand? It would take time after graduation before I fully understood how to bring these pieces together for a satisfactory solution. More to the point, for years I would find myself incessantly changing or adjusting a part of the composition so that it would have a more pleasing and meaningful result. However, back at Pratt in 1954, I had to wait another year before getting to what you might say, the real stuff, and learning how to create forms in space and time that were considered beautiful and benefitted people's lives. Along the way I learned what excited people, how they thought and acted and, perhaps, why they acted. Courses in sociology and aesthetics, history and literature helped. Technology and engineering that supported what I designed brought together talented people to make things matter.

Lincoln, Vietnam, Korea, Washington, Gettysburg. They touched a vein of understanding and often built on the visitor's sense of the events, however vague that sense might be. The memorial connects through an unspoken internal agreement to understand and empathize with those involved. In both, the significance of this person or this war touches the soul and stimulates the imagination.

The once ubiquitous "man-on-a-horse" has not been seen in new memorials for a long time. His time has passed. The horse too has vanished as a symbol of leaders. And we ourselves have changed. We view our deeds, the great ones and the failures, from a new perspective conditioned by our time. Here I can see anew, my connection to a moment.

I see the traditional sculpture of a person standing, such as Webster on a pedestal, or of a general sitting on a horse, arm gesturing—Longstreet sitting on his horse at Gettysburg has meant something to those who put it there. It belonged to their circle of understanding; it represented, through its image, the strength of those moments, perhaps the loss of that person—and with him, the loss of an era. Similarly, Rodin's *Burghers of Calais* at the Met brought meaning to me. I could immediately see the grieving.

That afternoon back in 2015, taking a moment at Lincoln's feet, I looked out at the expanse of the Mall. To the left is the Vietnam Memorial. On the right is the Korean War Veterans Memorial. Washington is ahead, standing tall. I imagined myself in August 1963, standing at the Lincoln Memorial, at the March on Washington for Jobs and Freedom, looking over the crowds that had assembled. I could clearly hear Martin Luther King say, "I have a dream."

The Medal of Honor & The Washington Monument

Let us pray as the day goes down
White gloves, polish, and flowers in the park

FIVE
GENERAL WASHINGTON AND THE DINNER

The Dinner was set for Sunday, June 20th, 1790 at Thomas Jefferson's New York City residence, 57 Maiden Lane, beginning at the fashionable hour of four o'clock in the afternoon. A white wine from France may have greeted the guests according to historian Charles Cerami. Invited were just two, Alexander Hamilton and James Madison.

Salad of Virginia Greens
Madeira Jelly Dressing

After a salad, a "capon stuffed with Virginia ham and chestnut puree, artichoke bottoms and truffles with a bit of cream," was followed by an "elegant beef stew."

Capon Stuffed with Virginia Ham
Chestnut Puree, Artichoke and Truffles
Calvados Sauce

Boeuf à la mode New York

"Meringues, macaroons, bell fritters" preceded a "delicious vanilla ice cream that still seemed like a miracle, for it was enclosed within a warm pastry, like a cream puff."

Vanilla Ice Cream Within a Warm Pastry
Meringues, Macaroons, Bell Fritters

During the courses, four other wines were served, including a red. The dinner ended with champagne without bubbles, which was enthusiastically received with great discussion about a certain grape from which this champagne was made. (Perhaps Jefferson had received a cut of the vine in his European travels, sent it home and had it planted in his Virginia vineyards, as was his habit to enhance his property with rare cuttings). With the wines, the conversation brightened in open discussion.

White wine Tains Doux et Liquoreux
Graves 1786
Montepulciano from Tuscany
Champagne Non-Mousseux

The happy circumstances of a delicious dinner and agreeable company satisfied more than one appetite. A deal was made that night that fulfilled both Hamilton's and Jefferson's deepest wishes. Madison had agreed to support Hamilton's financial ideas, helping to shift the few votes needed (yet, not changing his own vote! Still unsure?); in return Hamilton would back Jefferson's notion of placing the new United States capital in Virginia on the banks of the Potomac River, as related by historian Joseph Ellis. For this, the United States would have a banking system incorporating the federal government's assumption of the war debts of the colonies.

Today, because of these three men and one impatient president, we live within the result of this social and politically vibrant evening. With a handshake on the evening of the agreement, followed by the eventual vote from the Congress, Americans then and to this day, were catapulted into two new places, one a physical location that would become forever the political power-center of the world; and the other, a financial instrument and economic structure of strength that would surround us, support and protect us, at times, confuse us; and twice—1929 and post 9/11—play a supporting role in bringing us to the brink of economic disaster and then, its recovery.

Preceding this dinner meeting, there had been many months of discussion and arguments among the representatives of the states on the subjects of the payment of the colonies' now states' debts, as well as the location of the national Capitol (referred to as the "residence" question).

Jefferson, President Washington's Secretary of State, having returned from Paris directly to his Virginia home, had been kept informed by letters from James Madison. Apparently, he was in no hurry to join President Washington in New York. Hamilton, Washington's Secretary of the Treasury had completed an in-depth report on the Public Credit in January. He forwarded it to Congress where it was reviewed in detail and debated at length, particularly its provisions for funding. Madison, the floor leader of the House of Representative, had taken issue with some of the features in the funding of the domestic debt, mainly the reimbursement of the government securities owned by the citizens—some of which became complicated because the bonds were sold at a lesser price during the war to raise cash. Further, with the knowledge of the report, banking insiders and other speculators bought securities in anticipation of a handsome profit. While it was agreed that the capital would be either in New York City or Philadelphia, Hamilton was frustrated trying to convince Congress to adopt his financial plan for the federal government and to assume the state's war debts. He reasoned that adopting these debts, as part of his broad fiscal plan, would provide for a stable nation, one that was able to exhibit strength and be taken seriously in international relations and, importantly, to facilitate continuing to raise money.

Hamilton was a believer in a strong central federal government and admired the British system. He had Washington's support. Jefferson believed in states' rights, minimizing the power of a central federal government, keeping the power within the states. Ellis says there were "sharp differences dividing the leadership of the revolutionary generation: sectional versus national allegiance; agrarian versus commercial economic priorities...." And to make matters worse, Jefferson frequently would write brief notes to Washington exaggerating the threat of Hamilton wanting a return to the monarchy—which was untrue and angered the president. To further complicate matters, these disquieting vibrations at the start of the new country became known by many in the nation and in Europe's financial circles (which had been lending generously to the states during and after the war), potentially creating massive instability for Washington's presidency and his country's future.

In May, a month before the Jefferson and Hamilton dinner, President Washington fell dangerously ill with pneumonia. The doctors said it might be fatal. Jefferson finally realized the President was the leveling source of confidence in the country and in foreign money markets. He understood the risk of losing the support of the bankers in Britain, Switzerland, and the Netherlands during this young nation's period of uncertainty and decided he needed to change his reasoning and formulated a plan.

The day before the dinner, on June 19th, 1790, near President Washington's residence in lower Manhattan, Thomas Jefferson ran into a dejected Alexander Hamilton. Hamilton had been trying to get an agreement from the Congress about his plans for the nation's new fiscal system—particularly the assumption of the debts the colonies incurred during the War for Independence. Jefferson suggested they meet for dinner the following day at his residence.

He also invited James Madison to the dinner. Madison was Jefferson's close Virginian friend, and had kept the ambassador briefed about the many issues in Congress during Jefferson's five years in France. Madison was also leader of the congressional bloc that opposed Hamilton's banking plan. Having become friends while writing the Federalist Papers, Madison and Hamilton were now at odds over the assumption of the debt.

The new Secretary of State was a man of means, in spite of the fact that he had incurred huge debts. He had been Governor of Virginia during the Revolutionary War, not serving in the war, and was the sole owner of his mansion, Monticello, in Virginia. As for his New York City rental home, it was most certainly gracious, filled with fine European furniture, and decorated with an eye toward accommodating his friends, from both of New York's political and social worlds.

Adding to the drama of the evening, it appeared Jefferson had his sights on the US capital being located in Virginia, near his home. He also believed President Washington would agree to the proposal, as his home, Mount Vernon, was on the banks of the Potomac. Jefferson had something to trade and had brought together the right people for this dinner to make it happen.

The June 20th dinner was unquestionably one of the most important dinners in this nation's history.

I was aware of the Washington Monument for decades, seen in newspaper articles, photographs or mentioned in magazines. However, I first saw the monument while in the Army, stationed at Fort Meade, Maryland just outside Washington, DC. It was the early 1960s, and I was an Aviation Company Executive officer and a helicopter pilot with the 3rd Armored Cavalry Regiment, soon to be deployed to West Germany after a wall was built in Berlin. I saw it again, ten years later during the time of the Vietnam War, as I walked near its base in peace marches with a dear friend, Jim Mitchell, then on the senior staff of a client, and thousands of other like-minded citizens. A few years later, I marched with Judy Collins and thousands in support of women's rights. I was one in the ever-changing crowd of hundreds of thousands of visitors walking by this icon of America, known throughout the world. The Washington Monument seems to have always been there. Classic in its simplicity. Enduring. From a distance it captured me; up close, its immense scale made me feel only one of many. Yet proud. I felt an unbelievable sense of presence... and pride.

The Washington Monument is doubly resplendent for me and the Korean War Veterans Memorial. It became an anchor for this memorial, and similarly for the Vietnam Veterans Memorial— a point of alignment. Together with the Lincoln Memorial as a base, the four form an essential quadrilateral. Standing tall in times of peace and steady in the tumult of war, the Washington Monument marks the center of the National Mall, anchored at one end by the Nation's Capitol and at the other by the Lincoln Memorial and the Reflecting Pool. Since its inception, it has become the metaphoric backbone of this country.

In this indispensable role, had it not been for President Washington and his Secretaries of Treasury and State, we might never have had a National Mall and a place for Lincoln, Vietnam and Korea.

I realized I needed to know much more about George Washington. Remembering him mostly as the one who threw a silver dollar across the Potomac River (which I'm led to believe he never achieved) and, when he was a little boy, chopped down a cherry tree which didn't seem the necessary foundation for our nation's leader, less not telling a lie. I must have missed the class about the Battle of Brooklyn and other lessons. I had not known or forgot, that he had been in Brooklyn—not far from where I went to high school and college, near Fort Greene Park. Compelled to understand this man, I read from many sources, principally Ron Chernow's *Washington: A Life* and Joseph Ellis's *Founding Brothers*. In the spring and summer of 1776, two extraordinary events happened, one in a most expeditious period of time. A third, four years later.

First, the Continental Congress, meeting in Philadelphia, resolved to declare independence. To do so, they required that the colonies confirm the vote. Six colonies were still in question, New York, New Jersey, Pennsylvania, Delaware, Maryland and South Carolina. A final vote was delayed until July

1st when all the votes would be present. The word went out. Apparently, the matter was passed down from the legislatures to the town level, seemingly completing the debate yet extending the time for confirmation. Massachusetts alone (though not a colony in question) would have required fifty-eight town and county responses. However, within a month and a half, Congress had received an almost unanimous affirmation from the towns for independence (New York abstaining)—a "decidedly republican," "sweeping democratic" response, the likes of which, as Joseph J. Ellis writes, had never been tried before. Even so, I can't imagine the speed of moving this information and approvals back and forth between the Congress in Philadelphia and six of the Colonies, its cities, towns and hamlets, carried in pouches by messengers astraddle horses. Amazing! In one short month and a half, which included the time to meet and debate in each town and hamlet, the votes were received back in Philadelphia. Everyone wanted independence. I can only think of today, and Congress's seemingly snail-paced approvals, if there are approvals, with everyone in the same building, on their cell phones, texting and tweeting.

The second event started in England. George III, in 1776, dispatched a massive armada to cross the Atlantic—historically it would remain the largest fleet until 1917, more than 140 years later, when President Woodrow Wilson sent General John J. Pershing and the American Expeditionary Force in the opposite direction to support the British in Europe and fight in World War I. Under George III's direction, 150 ships with 42,000 troops—including Hessian mercenaries and Scottish Highlanders, plus others sent up from South Carolina and still others down from Halifax, Nova Scotia (the remnants of the Redcoats who had evacuated Boston after their bloody disgrace on Bunker Hill). All now met in waters off Staten Island, New York, at the mouth of the Hudson River, to defend the British Crown's hold of the colonies. In England, with the king's blessing, Lord George Germain, the British Secretary of State for the American colonies, appointed the Howe brothers—Richard, a Lord and admiral, and William a general, each with an extraordinary record of military achievement—to lead their forces and win back the colonies.

Earlier that same year, General Washington had led the Continental Army of 10,000 troops to Manhattan Island, New York. (Some writers say 19,000. The numbers don't seem to correspond from various sources. Congress had promised an additional 15,000 militia from the New England colonies). Upon seeing the lay of the land, Washington knew his troops could not defend this city, largely because of its complicated geography—three islands, one very large, the other two smaller, the narrow island surrounded by two rivers—and its strong loyalist population together with the impending arrival of the overwhelming British fleet. Yet, by nature, Washington pressed on.

A few months ago I stood on the observation floor atop the new World Trade Center, 101 & 102 levels above New York Harbor. I was designing the One World Explorer for the Tower and stepped to the massive windows where I could look down over the Harbor and the waters abutting Staten Island and Brooklyn. It was a thrilling sight, the miles of water surrounding the city below, the view on one side from the Statue of Liberty reaching up the west side of the Island along the Hudson River and the West Side Highway, past the George Washington Bridge, the map showing roads bending into Connecticut; and the other side looking down onto Governors Island, seeing the water flowing from Long Island Sound in the north-east into the East River, curving under the Triborough Bridge (now the Robert F. Kennedy Bridge) and Hell Gate under Manhattan's bridges into the Upper Bay, past Governors Island, eventually under the Verrazano Bridge and into the Atlantic Ocean. I visualized those 150 tall-mast ships of the English fleet, crowded into the now open waters of the Upper Bay... massive. Looking down at the East River, New York Harbor and the waters abutting Staten Island and Brooklyn, I could see the problem Washington had with this island city. As for me, I wondered about the space that each ship needed to swing at anchor twice a day when the tide changed and the treacherous currents shifted. The British ships were placed in a decidedly "imperial" massive position, according to Joseph J. Ellis; "true, each side was to the core values it claimed to be fighting for ... the coercive power of an empire against the consensual potency of a fledgling republic."

The battle started in late August 1776, on a warm New York day. With a clear vision that the British would overrun his positions in Brooklyn Heights, Washington, under cover of fog and threat of severe weather, led his army in the pre-dawn darkness from those encampments, across the East River, past the British ships, onto Manhattan Island, marching northward through what was then tree-covered hill and dale (today the crowded avenues and streets of the richly cosmopolitan East Side). After shooting engagements at Kip's Bay and Harlem Heights, the future president moved his troops forward to Fort Washington (now a largely residential area and a massive hospital complex), then on to King's Bridge, eventually arriving at White Plains in October 1776. By mid-November, with General Howe closing in, Washington turned, crossed the Hudson into New Jersey and marched down to Trenton, which led to his historic crossing of the Delaware River on the frozen Christmas night of 1776 to mount a significant attack and claim victory over Hessian and British positions. He saved his army for another day and was rewarded with the eventual victory over the superior British army at Yorktown, Virginia, in 1781—five years after the war began. Two years later, the 1783 Treaty of Paris, signed in Paris by King George of England and representatives of the United States of America ended the war. General Washington's brilliance was his ability to wait patiently to decide how best he could use his poorly equipped and outnumbered troops.

George Washington was strikingly tall and able to dominate a crowd with his self-assurance. He possessed a magnetic sense of leadership and a resolve to bring together the independent states; a monumental task for this individual who had championed over England, a seemingly superior nation, better equipped with guns and material while, at the time, a reluctant and withholding Congress seemed not to have listened to the needs of their troops for clothing and arms . . . and wages. General Washington successfully urged his troops to stay beyond their enlistment. He was the natural choice to be this new nation's president. Ellis tells us that Washington carried himself with formality and a sense of "cultivated aloofness . . . (that) contributed to his sense of majesty." The Revolution had demanded a single leader growing evermore into a singular commander. This dignity generated arguments in Congress in favor of addressing our country's first president as though he were royalty, "Your Highness"—ironic perhaps, given the hatred of the monarchs whom America had beaten into surrender.

    I have grown to admire George Washington, who, in my early way of thinking, seemed to pale in comparison with Jefferson, Franklin and Hamilton. During the Revolutionary War, General Washington, then greatly respected, had experienced little accommodation from the Congress. The delegates had put off the vote to provide him with the clothes, boots and weapons he needed for his Army, their Army. Yet, he prevailed. Now, years later, he was undoubtedly relieved that Congress had ceased their bickering.

Now for the third event, the important dinner, discussed earlier, undoubtedly the most important dinner of this time, perhaps even of this country's history. Learning of the dinner, I became enticed with the idea that there was an invisible finger from 1790 pointing to my place as a designer two hundred years later. All at once, the pieces of American history started to bring personal meaning in my mind, how there were stepping-stones from Maiden Lane in Lower Manhattan to the making of the National Mall and location of the Korean War Veterans Memorial and the Mural wall.

In the month following that eventful (and delicious-sounding!) dinner, after a long debate, Congress confirmed the residence for the new capital; it designated a diamond-shaped ten-mile square tract of land on the Potomac River. (Curiously, Ellis states that before the dinner, "the Potomac location for the permanent capital had, in fact, already been secured." However, he doesn't leave us with any details). Many in New York were incensed, as all hope was lost for their city, the financial and cultural capital of the nation, becoming its political center as well, similar to London and Paris. A smaller area within this diamond would become the city of Washington, the District of Columbia.

After the signing of the Treaty of Paris, Congress voted to put Washington in charge of the planning of the new capital. It was enlisting a powerful ally, a fine craftsmen both of strategy and architecture—not only a general who had led the young country in a successful war against one of the most powerful countries in the world, but also someone who had continued building and refurbishing his Mount Vernon estate on the Potomac. President Washington was a force to be reckoned with. It was felt that he would master the design, oversee the process, and add his own eminence to the project. He asked Major Pierre Charles L'Enfant, a friend from his Revolutionary War days, to design the site of the nation's capital and draw up the plan. L'Enfant's design featured ceremonial spaces and avenues radiating out from two building sites, one for Congress, the other for the President, soon to be called the White House. L'Enfant envisioned an uninterrupted green space, which eventually would become the National Mall and the center for a nation honoring its war veterans, leaders and presidents, and its iconic events.

During these months, President Washington spent time planning the construction of a canal. Ellis writes that Washington believed the Potomac

River was a direct link to a "river system of the interior . . . he knew in his bones that the energy of the American people must flow in that direction." It would be the task of Thomas Jefferson, Washington's Secretary of State, when he became President, to effect the Louisiana Purchase in 1803 from France, expanding the country westward, eventually authorizing Lewis and Clark to explore one of its principal river systems, the Missouri, to its headwaters in the western mountains.

George Washington died on December 14, 1799. Nine days after his death, John Marshall, who later became Chief Justice of the Supreme Court, proposed a tomb to be constructed in the capital as a memorial. The family, however, declined to move Washington's body from a tomb on his estate in Virginia. His body would remain at Mount Vernon while disagreement about the kind of memorial as well as the lack of funds continued to delay the next step in this memorial process.

America in the end would have to wait some thirty-one years—until 1832, the 100th anniversary of Washington's birth—for the Washington National Monument Society to be formed. The committee laid out their vision for a memorial and in September 1835, a competition for the memorial was finally announced. The competition specified:

> *It is proposed that the contemplated monument shall be like [Washington] in whose honor it is to be constructed . . . it should blend stupendousness with elegance, and be of such magnitude and beauty as to be an object of pride to the American people. . . . Its material is intended to be wholly American, and to be of marble and granite brought from each state, that each state may participate in the glory of contributing material as well as in funds to its construction.*
>   —Washington National Monument Society. September 1835

A perfect design assignment!

Four years later, Robert Mills was selected as the architect. Mills was born in Charleston, South Carolina, in 1781. A Freemason, as was George Washington, Mills was arguably the first native-born American to become a professional architect.

His design called for a 600-foot obelisk—almost as we see the monument today. And, it was to be surrounded by a circular colonnade, and on top, a sculpture of Washington standing in a chariot drawn by a team of horses!

Both the price tag—21 million in today's dollars—and criticism of the design caused the leaders of the Monument Society to delay the whole project. Finally, they authorized the building of the obelisk in 1848, but postponed the construction of the colonnade. To raise funds, according to a report by the United States Army Corps of Engineers, they decided that states, organizations, foreign countries, citizens, and Native American tribes would donate "memorial stones that could be fitted into the interior walls." Only then did the project move forward—but not before a controversy regarding the sponsorship and inscription of the donated stones was settled.

A donation from Pope Pius IX infuriated anti-Catholics. The "Know Nothing" party boycotted and eventually took control of the Monument Society, maintaining their management of it until 1858 when money ran out. Congress authorized further funds. However, the Civil War caused delays yet again. The war ended, and under Ulysses S. Grant, Congress took control of the monument. The design was reconsidered; they chose to retain Mill's concept, but to refine the obelisk to a more classic proportion with an apex. The redesign was undertaken by Thomas Lincoln Casey of the Corps of Engineers, with construction resuming in 1879.

Thomas Lincoln Casey had attended West Point and graduated first in the class of 1852. He taught engineering at the military academy, and later served during the Civil War, in charge of the coastal fortifications in Maine. After the war he became head of the Office of Public Buildings and Grounds in the District of Columbia. When he redesigned the monument, he also undertook the re-engineering of the foundation, which needed strengthening. Once it was completed, and with additional Congressional funding, he was able to turn to the construction of the upper two-thirds of the Monument. However, by that time, the original quarry stone curiously could not be found, or was not available. As a result, the stone in the new construction was slightly darker than the bottom third. It's still apparent when I first looked at the Monument and again today, 140 years later. A third stone from a Maryland quarry was found and used to complete the construction. The capstone was placed in 1884, eighty-five years after Washington's death. The colonnade and the chariot were thankfully abandoned altogether.

The apex of the obelisk is cast from aluminum—the world's most expensive metal at that time. Engraved on one side of the apex are the words *Laus Deo* (Praise be to God). Two other sides give the dates of the laying of the capstone and corner stones, and the names of the Joint Commission: Chester

A. Arthur; W. W. Corcoran, Chairman; M. E. Bell; Edward Clark; John Newton (Not the slave ship captain who had a spiritual experience, changed his life for the better and wrote *"Amazing Grace"!* Maybe a namesake?). On the fourth side are the names of Chief Engineer and Architect: Thos. Lincoln Casey, Colonel, Corps of Engineers; Assistants: George W. Davis, Captain, 14th Infantry, Bernard R. Green, Civil Engineer, and the Master Mechanic, P. H. McLaughlin. Robert Mills's name and credit as the original architect and designer had been omitted. A disappointment.

It's now April 6, 2017, and I've just returned home from hearing the glorious *War Requiem* by Benjamin Britten at the Cathedral St. John the Divine. A thrilling performance by the Cathedral Choristers, the Manhattan School of Music Chamber Choir, the Manhattan School of Music Symphonic Choir, the Manhattan School of Music Symphony Orchestra and the Oratorio Society of New York, all under the baton of Kent Tritle.

What an apt time to hear Britten's masterpiece as we were recovering from news of Syria's President al-Assad again dropping sarin gas on his people, killing eighty and creating untold physical injury to many others, infants to elders—people suddenly not being able to breathe, struggling to get enough oxygen as their friends and family showered them with water to wash away the remnants of this nerve gas.

Britten composed *War Requiem* in 1961 to consecrate the rebuilding of the cathedral at Coventry, England, after the Nazis had destroyed it during WWII. The decade in which he created the work was one of global unrest with the erection of the Berlin Wall, the Cuban Missile Crisis, and the escalation of the Vietnam War, each unfolding in seemingly rapid succession; not to mention the Korean War was in a stand-off, hostilities having ceased just eight years earlier.

Throughout the concert, I sat transfixed, listening for nearly two hours to the choirs and orchestras and the three soloists—soprano, baritone and tenor—sing, at times, with the joined choirs; at other times, solo, softly and then with passion as the orchestras grew in prominence. Behind us, at the far west end of the Cathedral, the Boys' Choir, composed of boys and girls, sung in answer to the main choir standing behind the orchestras, extending into the choir area east of the Cathedral central crossing.

As I listened, my thoughts bounced, from England in 1940 to what I was doing in Europe as Britten was composing the piece, to the significance of the Korean War. I looked at the talented members of the orchestra seated only fifteen feet away—the twenty or thirty or more violinists and violas. All young musicians, mostly Asian—perhaps even Korean . . . so removed from the conflicts on the Asian peninsula and in Syria and their aftermath; so removed from all those decisions made in the 1940s and 50s at Yalta and Potsdam that impacted lives in Korea, Central and Eastern Europe, the Middle East and other parts of the world for generations to come. So, perhaps not so far removed. There is much evidence each day that the struggle goes on.

As I have known, but particularly after that night of the concert, music is a metaphor for peace and cooperation. For without it, there is chaos and hatred. It is through music and art and painting and design that we are brought together to better know one another and enjoy ourselves. No one understood this more clearly than Washington, a great music enthusiast—he loved to dance the minuet—used to bemoan the "music of the army," saying it was "in general very bad."

I can still hear the tenor and baritone sing Britten's closing. The Tenor, "It seems that out of battle I escaped/Down some profound dull tunnel . . ." He ends, "Strange friend . . . here is no cause to mourn." The Baritone answers, "None" . . . "save the undone years, the hopelessness." Eventually the Baritone says, "I am the enemy you killed, my friend . . . as you jabbed and killed. I parried; but my hands were loath and cold. . . . Let us sleep now. . . ." The baritone and Tenor sing, "Let us sleep now." Then, the Boys sing, "Lord, grant them eternal rest, and let the perpetual light shine upon them." Finally the Chorus sings, "Let them rest in peace. Amen."

The entire Cathedral was enveloped in silence. When the conductor's arms finally fell to his sides, the audience erupted. I stood with all in endless applause and gratitude.

Twenty-five years earlier, I thought of the sun rising behind the Washington Monument, the locus, the choral alignment for the Korean War Veterans Memorial; it is the place where the sun rises to illuminate each and every one of those thousands of portraits of men and women on the mural wall, which stands on grounds ordained in New York in 1790 by three forward-thinking leaders of a new government and its first president.

Abraham Lincoln (Profile)

March the main streets and the boulevards
On a Veteran's Day
On a Veteran's Day

SIX
THE STRUGGLE FOR THE LINCOLN MEMORIAL

"So long as I live, I'll never let a memorial to Abraham Lincoln be erected in that goddamned swamp," Joseph Gurney Cannon said in 1902, then the most powerful Chairman of the House Appropriations Committee, eventually to become the all-powerful Speaker of the House.

⁓⁓

In the midst of a 1992 design meeting with the Korean War Veterans Memorial Advisory Board, Jim McKevitt, a member of the Board, pulled me aside and asked if I had seen the cellar archives of the Lincoln Memorial. He suggested I look into the history of its design, saying I would be astonished by its process. It seemed important then. I made note of it and quickly refocused on the mural design, coordinating with my staff and Frank Gaylord's nineteen sculptures, planned to be in front of the mural.

Until the morning of the Korean War Veterans Memorial's dedication, Lincoln was a mirage to me, save for the moments I visited him before this commission, while serving in the Army and later moments when consulting on design projects with the Information Agency (USIA), the Food and Drug Administration (FDA) and other agencies. But on July 27th, 1995, with tears in my eyes as I looked at the Korean mural with Frank's soldiers mirrored in its brilliant polished finish, I also saw the reflection of the Lincoln Memorial and McKevitt's words rang in my ears. Nevertheless, five more years would pass before I had time to turn to Lincoln and uncover the tale behind its design.

By September 2000, Jim McKevitt was gone, and I was on my own to dig into the history that he had once referred. Having known McKevitt, I had no doubt that I would learn something new. And did I ever!

According to the story it took more than twenty years for the Lincoln Memorial to become a reality. The process would wind its way through five presidents (William McKinley, Theodore Roosevelt, William Howard Taft, Woodrow Wilson and Warren G. Harding), three architects (Charles McKim, Henry Bacon and John Russell Pope), two Commissions of Fine Art, and three design competitions. More importantly, it would play a role in where and why the Korean War Veterans Memorial would be placed.

In 1898, for the centennial celebration of the nation's capital, Congress approved a program to rejuvenate Pierre L'Enfant's original 1791 plan. L'Enfant, working with President George Washington, had envisioned broad avenues and a central landscaped area to symbolically define the government and states of this new country. However, over time, the park had become marred with railroad crossings and a rail station. Slums and houses of prostitution had grown up around the Capitol. A commission, named for Senator James McMillan, was set up to correct this.

Formed in 1901, the McMillan Commission was composed of the visionary designers of the day—planner Daniel Burnham, architect Charles F. McKim, sculptor Augustus Saint-Gaudens and landscape architect Frederick Law Olmsted, Jr. (Olmsted's father, Frederick Law Olmsted was the renowned landscape designer of the time and founding father of American landscape architecture; he designed the Biltmore Estate landscape in Asheville, the Capitol space earlier in 1874 and with Calvert Vaux, designed New York City's Central Park). Burnham, the farsighted strategist of Chicago's 1893 World's Columbian Exposition, would chair the Commission, while Charles F. McKim would be the driving design force. He called for a broad green mall starting at the Capitol, moving west, encompassing the Washington Monument and extending through marshlands to the Potomac River. (The marshlands were to be filled from the dredging of the Potomac that was scheduled to make the river more navigable for the deeper draft ships). The Mall would end in a dramatic design for a Lincoln Memorial as the strong western anchor of the plan and include a Memorial bridge across the Potomac to Virginia, eventually leading to Arlington Cemetery, the location of the Tomb of the Unknown Soldier and the final resting place of more than four hundred thousand of the nation's war dead. In essence, encompassing all of the National Mall area extending across the Potomac River that we are so familiar with today.

McKim's Lincoln Memorial was the brilliant part of the McMillan Plan presented to President Theodore Roosevelt at the Corcoran Gallery in January 1902, to grand acclaim. It had the President's overwhelming support. However, Washington and the country would have to wait.

"Not for another ten years, until 1912, would action on the Lincoln Memorial be decisive, and even then a final fight lay ahead in Congress," writes historian Christopher Thomas. Joe Cannon, the House Appropriations Committee Chair, "despised the McMillan Plan."

With piercing dark eyes, stern thin-lips, a closely cut, white beard, a determined, slim-face, and wearing his preferred black bow tie, Cannon had a pugnacious overbearing manner, and ruled with an iron hand, exercising his power in a partisan manner. A tyrant, in other words. In the early years of his career, he was referred to as "Foul Mouth Joe," though later his moniker was softened to "Uncle Joe." Staunchly conservative, he espoused a "practical" fiscal policy; he was reactionary and opposed most progressive measures, cautioning against government spending—"not one cent on scenery," Uncle Joe admonished. Resources say he was referring to "environmental concerns", specifically the environmental concerns of President Theodore Roosevelt. I suspect he meant not one cent for beautiful and attractive features. Now in charge of the national budget, he had authority over the expenditures for the memorial.

It was at this time, when presented with the proposed Lincoln Memorial, that Uncle Joe said, he would never let a memorial to Abraham Lincoln be built in "that goddamned swamp." He proceeded to foster an astounding series of discussions and arguments, then unique to Congress and Washington, on the subject of design and city planning.

Joe Cannon wasn't opposed to honoring President Lincoln per se. Early in his career he was a follower of Lincoln during the Lincoln-Douglas debates. Cannon was a Republican as was Lincoln. However, he and the House of

Representatives had been bypassed during the McMillan Commission's design process and concurrent authorization of the memorial. Furthermore, Cannon justified his disapproval, saying its placement in the Potomac marshes represented the new, expansive, nationalizing "Rooseveltianism" that he disliked. Thus, in addition to the Potomac marsh, he placed two new sites for the memorial under consideration: Meridian Hill in Washington and the other in the form of a highway named after Abraham Lincoln that would run from Washington to Gettysburg, with memorial arches symbolizing the emerging automobile via the popular Henry Ford.

In the meantime, McMillan had died, as had McKim. For legal and political reasons, Roosevelt's successor, President William Howard Taft, established a new Commission of Fine Arts. This gave rise to a new Lincoln Memorial Commission, which Taft chaired. This was a new level of importance for art and design in the national political landscape. President Taft became a national advocate for design with this new Fine Arts Commission and he strategically included Joe Cannon in the Arts Commission. Yet Uncle Joe remained unconvinced that the Lincoln Memorial should be at the western end of the National Mall in the Potomac marshes. He had already lost a bid for his Lincoln Memorial idea as part of the new Union Station. A competition was opened to explore both sites: the Potomac marshes and Meridian Hill. (The Lincoln Memorial Highway idea had diminished as a contender, yet it would continually be raised as the two other sites were being deliberated. After some investigation, it seems that it was never a serious contender but more a reflection of the fashionably new automotive technology, given it would only have been used by auto owners. Mostly, it appeared, a strip of concrete just could not compete with an alluring sculpture of Lincoln himself).

It was reasoned that an architect who had worked with McKim was the obvious selection as the architect for the Potomac site. Henry Bacon, then forty-four years old, was chosen. He had a fine reputation but was not known in Washington. Daniel Burnham, the former planner of the McMillan Commission, and now the Chair of Washington's Fine Arts Commission, had known him for two decades, particularly when Bacon was in Chicago as McKim's representative during the design of the World's Fair in 1893. He supported Bacon's candidacy saying that this architect was "a man not of actual achievement but of supreme promise" and "would put his very life into [this] task." A curious recommendation, but with that said, Burnham would soon die, after having designed the new Union Station as part of the McMillan Plan. Meanwhile John Russell Pope had been selected in Burnham's place to design the Meridian Hill site.

The design process was restarted. Bacon's design direction followed McKim's concept of a memorial to Lincoln as a symbol of the Union, showing his warm humanity. He prepared three related directions for the memorial with variations on the openness of the building enclosure and the placement of the sculpture (including one proposal setting it outside) as well as its gestures.

Pope's direction, on the other hand, focused on Lincoln's personal openness and kindness; the design featured an open rotunda showing a sculpture similar to the serene *Standing Lincoln* previously created by Augustus Saint-Gaudens in 1887 for Lincoln Park in Chicago. Seeing reproductions of dark black and white sketches with Lincoln's drooped head and outstretched arms, I shiver at the design's ominous character—Christopher Thomas, the historian, describes it as "dramatic but somewhat menacing." I must agree!

With the aid of a publicity campaign for the Potomac site pressing for support, the highway idea was finally dropped for good. Pope's design, in the meantime, was criticized because of the inclusion of an immense Lincoln sculpture. At last, Bacon's design was selected as the most suitable—although he was asked to further refine his design before it was presented to Congress.

Today, I'm looking at photographs of Charles McKim's early renderings and model. I'm struck by the simplicity and final realization achieved by Bacon's plan—a design I've loved so much across the years. It reflects McKim's early concept yet sets its own theme and creative direction for the honesty and details in the architecture and the successful collaboration with the sculptor, Daniel Chester French, and his seated Abraham Lincoln. It is undoubtedly this partnership that makes the Lincoln Memorial so successful.

Bacon had conceived Lincoln seated, a tradition of the time for sculptures of dead statesmen. He chose Jules Guérin to prepare presentation renderings of the memorial and later retained him to paint the two large murals on the upper parts of the interior walls that are often overlooked by the visitors. He took extreme care in providing symbolic allegory. Thomas says,

"He filters ancient models through a screen of neoclassical precedents of the eighteenth and early nineteenth centuries." Built into his design, Bacon provided symbols of the nation in 1865: early drawings of the east elevation shows thirteen steps, each engraved with names of one of the first states to ratify the Constitution; thirty-six columns to remember the reunited states of the Union after the Civil War; wreaths of Northern laurel intertwined with Southern pine; selections from Lincoln's speeches; materials and details reminiscent of Greek refinements. He paid particular attention to the subtle variations of the color of the marble between the columns and modeled the floor and ceiling on Roman temple proportions. Bacon called the Lincoln Memorial a "temple."

In February 1916 upon being reelected to Congress, Joe Cannon went to the floor, turned to the House and stated clearly, he was wrong to have opposed the monument location. "We 'tenderfeet'. . . perhaps ought not to have our way in matters of art . . . Looking through the hindsight, I am inclined to think the Art Commission and the majority of the Memorial Commission located this memorial where it ought to be located."

On May 30, 1922, fifty-seven years after Lincoln's death and twenty-one years after the initial concepts of McKim, William Howard Taft, now president of the Memorial Commission and Chief Justice of the United States, dedicated the Lincoln Memorial.

Walking up the long series of steps of the Lincoln Memorial, I see Lincoln slowly emerge from the darkness inside his temple. First his head; next his eyes gazing into the distance; then the fullness of his face, his solemn expression denoting strength; then his body, his hands resting on the arms of his chair. I approach slowly, looking up at him, chiseled in white marble, sitting in a chair in a building surrounded by his ideas: his Gettysburg Address is on the wall to the left; his Second Inaugural Address to the right; behind him, is the Dedication. I stand in silence, knowing him better since I first came here decades ago, late on a warm summer night when his presence glowed brilliant white. Knowing the tragedy of the loss of his life, and the 750,000 casualties in four years of civil war—a dear price to keep our Union together, I sense this pain. I see the subtle nuances that give meaning and bring grandeur to this place.

When I think of the Lincoln Memorial, I mostly envision the sculpture of Lincoln, the President. Daniel Chester French was at the height of his career when his long-time friend, Henry Bacon, selected him in 1913 to be the sculptor for the memorial. French had completed an array of highly recognized sculptures including his earliest work, *Minute Man* in Concord, Massachusetts, the popular *Alma Mater* at Columbia University in New York City, a standing *Abraham Lincoln* in Lincoln, Nebraska to name just a few. The following year, French was formally appointed by the Lincoln Commission. Assuredly, he was America's leading sculptor at that moment, as well as Chairman of the Fine Arts Commission in Washington, succeeding Burnham in 1912. Initially he considered turning down the Lincoln commission, choosing instead to remain the Arts Commission's chair. But pressed by Bacon, he soon changed his mind and accepted the commission, remaining Chair of the Fine Arts Commission for three months and then resigned.

French originally understood the sculpture was to be cast in bronze, and so he penciled marble into his contract. The contract, however, was never amended. But Bacon, too, had conceived the sculpture to be in white marble—and ten feet tall. After many mock-ups, both men decided Lincoln should be nineteen feet tall instead—dramatically increasing the cost of the carving by more than three and a half times. Amazingly, in December 1917, the Commission amended the terms. The sculptor and the architect had prevailed.

How I wish I could have listened in on their conversations, the back and forth between the architect and the sculptor... and the approving commission. I could only imagine. I know how Frank Gaylord and I spoke to each other, no long conversations, lots of thoughts before speaking, nods and raised eyebrows, a movement of the head, some grunts, short statements mostly in agreement. At times, a smile from Frank. It was that sense of tacit understanding between two creative artists, both on the same page and sharing a common purpose.

Years ago, I learned that every public memorial's design and construction had been fraught with bureaucratic difficulties, not the least of which was getting paid! It was no different it seems for Bacon and French. Daniel Chester French had apparently written to Bacon about the profit French assumed Bacon was making. According to Michael Richman's monograph on French, Bacon replied in August of 1919:

> *Where in the world did you hear that I had made a half million out of the Lincoln Memorial? Of all the works I have ever engaged in, this memorial has been the most unprofitable financially. It is over eight years since I started on the drawings, the Government does not allow my traveling expenses to Washington, which have been on an average, I should say, once every ten days for the eight years, the cost of the drawings and models have been abnormally high, furthermore the red tape and officiousness of some of the bureaucrats in Washington has been incalculable in cost to my temper, and finally I wish to have nothing more to do with any government work whatever under present conditions . . . Selah!*

Of course, it had all been worth it and I think Bacon and French would agree. They had made a magnificent work of art, beautiful and timeless. But—paid on time, they should have been!

Standing inside the Memorial, I read the last few words of his Gettysburg Address, the thoughts after that terrible battle . . . *that we here highly resolve that these dead shall not have died in vain—that this nation, under God, shall have a new birth of freedom—and that government of the people, by the people, for the people, shall not perish from the earth.* The words draw me back to Gettysburg, eighty-five miles away, which I visited in June 2002.

On a bus from the Army War College at Carlisle, Pennsylvania, I rode with others, each with their own expectations of the historic site. I had attended a National Security Seminar at the War College in 2002. Those in the bus with me were Lt Colonels and Colonels in the Army, one from the Navy and a number of civilians, each a distinguished leader in his or her profession. Outside the window, I could see many small concrete markers as we approached this hallowed ground. I was ready to take photos after getting off the bus near the top of the site of Pickett's Charge. I grew quiet, as did the other passengers. The guide's comments seemed so far away. Soon a somber cloud covered me.

I walked away to be alone and not part of this group of twenty to thirty students from the Army War College. Almost paralyzed, I couldn't take a photograph across this long plain of death. I didn't know those Union or Confederate soldiers, but I could feel their presence. The silence and sadness enveloped me, as if the past had come rushing in.

On the afternoon of July 3, 1863, the third and last day of the battle, this place—now quiet in the light drizzle turning to a mist—was a living hell. Over 4,000 soldiers fell here in less than an hour. Other statistics say 7,000. In the 3 days at Gettysburg, 50,000 Americans, North and South, became casualties, injured or killed. We were told that on that day, you could not walk on dry ground for the blood of the dead and wounded.

Atop Cemetery Ridge, I could see a statue of the Union Major General George Meade on horseback looking down the slope, it seemed, toward a statue of the Confederate General Robert E. Lee—who had given the orders for the disastrous and deadly charge. To the left of Meade's gaze, General Longstreet is astride his steed behind the cannons at the edge of the woods. I noticed that there was no statue of Pickett.* Perhaps that's immaterial; the general and his troops would be forever remembered on this field. That is the fundamental thing Gettysburg does—it ties a string around our cultural finger, completes a circle and gives meaning to our collective feelings of loss.

Today I appreciate even more what that moment means beyond the immortalized images of the generals who presided over the charge. And here, in juxtaposition, across the 85 miles from Gettysburg to the National Mall, Lincoln sits.

Thankfully, the plains at Gettysburg are intact. Only the markers are in evidence across these fields. The town itself has been built up with limited commercial signage, not visible from the National Park. The nearby roads and highways have been paved, and the traffic on these pikes emitting a smooth quiet whir seems an anachronism in this hallowed space.

---

*Asking the Army War College why there was no statue of Pickett, I was informally told by one of their scholars that the South had decided not to honor General Pickett at this site because for years after Gettysburg, Pickett continuously held the unanimously admired General Lee responsible for the dramatic loss of his division and the lives of honored southern men.

In November 1863, a dedication at Gettysburg was scheduled. David Wills, who lived in Gettysburg, invited President Lincoln to be his guest; Wills had planned the ceremony and had made arrangements for the land, interring the dead and securing the Scotland-trained landscape architect William Saunders to design the cemetery grounds. David McConaughy, another lawyer in Gettysburg, had initiated efforts for a National Cemetery, while Wills chose the orator Edward Everett to give the principle address. Lincoln was asked to deliver "a few appropriate remarks."

Two days before the ceremony, Saunders was asked to show his plans to the President in Washington. Lincoln took great interest in the special circular arrangement of the graves radiating from a center point; unusual for gravesites of that era that were strictly aligned in straight rows and columns. The battle dead during the Civil War were so numerous, some cemeteries required mass burial in long, straight trenches, as in the Salisbury National Cemetery, North Carolina. Randolph Rogers, an American who had studied in Italy, was chosen as the sculptor for the tall central feature of the cemetery, which would become the Soldiers' Monument. Caspar Buberl, who studied in Prague and Vienna, was chosen as the sculptor for the New York State Monument, crowning Cemetery Hill. The State of New York had lost the greatest number of soldiers at Gettysburg, almost 6,700 of the 23,049 Union casualties.

At the dedication of the Soldier's National Cemetery, President Lincoln made his historic address—one that is remembered, memorized and repeated by school children and most grownups in this country and the world. His "few appropriate remarks," written while in transit on the 80-mile train ride from Washington to the hallowed ground of Gettysburg, are immortalized in our hearts and minds. They also appear, celebrated on the walls of his memorial on the National Mall.

> *Four score and seven years ago, our fathers brought forth on this continent a new nation, conceived in liberty and dedicated to the proposition that all men are created equal...*

This horrific Civil War ended, nineteen months after Lee left Gettysburg. On February 6, 1865, Confederate President Davis promoted Robert E. Lee commander of all the Confederate forces. Gettysburg was the turning point of the War Between the States, and two months after his promotion, Lee surrendered to General Ulysses S. Grant at Appomattox Court House in April.

A thought about Thomas Jefferson is appropriate here, for the memorials to Lincoln and Jefferson are so similar in concept, a distant walk away; yet so different in their brightness and splendor. Standing inside the Thomas Jefferson Memorial I read:

> We hold these truths to be self-evident: that all men are created equal; that they are endowed by their Creator with certain inalienable rights: that among these are life, liberty and the pursuit of happiness, that to secure these rights, governments are instituted among men . . .

As I walk up the steps and enter the memorial, situated across the Tidal Basin from the White House and Lincoln, *Jefferson* stands tall above me. Cast in a dark bronze, he is sheltered in an open round pavilion, looking west over the waters toward the White House. The memorial was commissioned at the insistence of Franklin Delano Roosevelt and placed so that the president could see it from the Oval Office. As I strain, do I see the hint of a smile on *Jefferson*'s lips? Supposedly, he, in turn, is looking toward FDR, but if you ask me his gaze is actually a bit further to the right, toward the Treasury Building and Alexander Hamilton, his adversary nevertheless, colleague in 1790.

Visiting the memorial, I have always felt *Jefferson* appears confined in his memorial space; too tall, almost black, perhaps not welcoming. His writing on the wall has lost its contrast, darkening with time, not easily readable—although in some photos (probably taken with a wide-angle lens and additional lighting) his writing appears more legible, with more space surrounding Jefferson. As beautiful and striking as it is, for me the interior doesn't have the graceful light feeling of the Lincoln Memorial. Jefferson's pavilion was designed by John Russell Pope in 1935-36. (Pope had been the runner-up in the Lincoln Memorial competition.) However, he died August 27, 1937, a year and a half before the construction started. As for Jefferson's sculpture, the memorial's Commission selected Rudolph Evans in 1941, four years after Pope's death. And due to a shortage of metals during the Second World War,

Evans created Jefferson in plaster with a finish to appear bronze-like. The sculpture was installed and dedicated on April 13, 1943, the 200th anniversary of Jefferson's birth. After WWII, when materials became more available, the sculpture was finally cast in bronze in 1947. As best as I can ascertain, with Pope's death, he and Evans never worked together, never talked or discussed the size of the sculpture as it relates to the proportions of the building, or the lighting or the patina on the bronze. They never had a chance. Perhaps there was some collaboration between Evans's and Pope's successors. However, as I see it, because of this separation between the two creators, the architect and the sculptor, the net effect has grown dark and tight over the years. With the Lincoln Memorial, Bacon and French worked very closely. It shows.

When I visit Lincoln, I bring new experiences that expand my sense of him and the leadership he exerted during his time and the Civil War. Skipping over Andrew Johnson, I think of General Ulysses S. Grant, who would soon assume the presidency, and Mathew Brady whose photographs indelibly captured the dead and dying and how they were cared for. I think of Walt Whitman who was drawn to help those in the hospitals. I've read about Frederick Law Olmsted, selected by Rev. Henry Bellows to be General Secretary of the US Sanitary Commission, bringing quality health care to Civil War soldiers, a significant step toward the beginning of an organized health service, before he became America's leading landscape architect. I read of Lincoln's time and gained a further understanding of the meaning of true leadership and an appreciation for the price paid to keep a nation together. In many photographs of Lincoln seated up high on a pedestal, individuals standing in front of the sculpture look tiny and unimportant. Personally, I never felt small and unimportant looking up at him. Nor as I read his words on the wall to his left and right. In contrast, I felt honored and enriched to be in his presence, grateful and strengthened as I walk down the steps and onto the Mall.

My visit to Gettysburg and the Army War College brings another insight to my visits to the Lincoln Memorial. Each and every aspect reaches across time, focuses on the National Mall and through the Korean War Veterans Memorial, centers on the Korea of 1950-1953 in contrast to the Korea of today.

This memorial place is a specially designed environment, concentrating the energy from all those connected by the life and the event. All those known and unknown, near or far, become brothers and sisters for me to share in their thoughts and energy. To remember. To heal. To understand. And to leave, renewed in my own life and rededicated to the principles for which they died.

Three Soldiers

The Sky tries smiling
Painted up, dry leaves flying
I can't stop wishing a rainbow

SEVEN
THE RIFT IN THE VIETNAM MEMORIAL

It was a joyless, cloudy day when I first came to visit the Vietnam Memorial Wall. Soon after its dedication in November 1982, I gazed at the hallowed, engraved names of those who had died in that conflict—so many names, increasing as I walked down the long black granite wall. I knew the story of a war that seemed to go on and on, a war that had been the backdrop for my own young years. After 1975 when Vietnam's nightmare was over, the conflict for the memorial for that war went on and on as well.

When I was selected to design the Mural to remember Korea's men and women, I visited the Vietnam Memorial again and again, to reflect, to mourn, to pay my everlasting respect.

The names. A few listed near the ground at the beginning of the wall. 1959, the beginning of America's loss of lives—before we called it a war. Today some historians designate Vietnam's conflict started in 1945, at the close of World War II. Others list it as 1955. Each time I return, I walk down the narrow footpath along a long black triangular wall. The few names at my feet quickly grow to hundreds. Then thousands. Now the names are above my head, overwhelming at the apex, 1975 marking the end of the war. The wall sharply turns to the right, the date 1959 engraved high up on the wall. The path now leads up the slope, alongside this second identical triangular wall, engraved with more names. Eventually, as of May 2017, 58,318 are listed on these two walls. 58,318 Americans killed. 58,318 not here today.

Jan C. Scruggs, a wounded and decorated Vietnam War veteran, envisioned a memorial dedicated to those who had served in Vietnam. Scruggs was in an infantry brigade during the war, and after his discharge, completed graduate studies at the American University in Washington, DC. He wanted to honor the veterans of the war and believed a memorial would bring healing to cure the national crisis caused by the long and controversial hostilities. It was 1979. He proceeded to establish a foundation, raised funds (starting with $2,800 of his own money), and obtained congressional authorization as well as a valuable piece of dedicated land on the National Mall. He knew what he wanted in a design competition, and it was he who insisted that a list of names of those who died in the war be one of its requirements. It seemed only natural, a part of a long tradition.

✦

Standing from afar, I see the design, a triangular-shaped black granite wall sloping downhill, joined by another triangular-shaped granite wall going back up the hill—two sunken black walls of names of those lost in battle, forming a "V"... a "rift in the earth," Maya Lin said. Depressed into the level green lawn, this is an abstraction, a metaphor for the depths of shame of this war.

The back face of the wall is supporting a wall of earth, where one can stand above and look down on the visitors who are looking at the names. Up here on the grass lawn, a light breeze blows as an American flag near the entrance ripples on this summer day. Lin's original concept did not include the flag.

This shockingly simple design for the memorial became highly controversial, not only because the war was controversial, but also the design was unfamiliar, a significant departure from traditional approaches as well as decades away from the "man-on-a-horse." Controversial because the designer was a young Asian-American woman, born in Ohio. The controversy over the Vietnam Veterans Memorial was hot, boiling, and fought right out there in public. It was called the "Art War."

The Vietnam War echoed in my mind for years. I was working at my design office during the war and through the controversy. Long hours, usually every day, and many weekends. At some moment, something clicked. Thinking back when I was a pilot in the Army, when, but for those two hours completing my qualification of 10 hours to fly the Huey, I could have been sent there, to Vietnam in '61 or '62; my name could have been on this wall.

This war hit my eyes each day in the papers and at the end of each day on the evening news, penetrating my thoughts and the vision of many Americans here and others living in countries far away. The war was divisive, the subject of protest marches and arguments at parties and in bars, over phone conversations and on the TV. Despising this war, I went to marches in Washington, DC, protesting the war, while honoring those who died in the war, and those who returned from the war. I reviled the curses and taunts of the protesters against the drafted soldiers who were sent to fight the war...and who returned, many broken. I understand many of those stories of vets being taunted or cursed (or help us, spat upon) were over blown and in many cases not proven. I loathed the positions being taken by the President and his cabinet. We lost JFK, RFK and Martin Luther King, Jr. in those years, along with all those youngsters in the war. I could not fly the ensign on my sailboat until we were out of Vietnam, a minor protest, yet it meant something to me. For nearly five years when in the Service, I had been one of them, ready to fight in West Germany if the Soviets came blasting over the Fulda Gap. Later, all the controversy surrounding the Vietnam Veterans Memorial was, for me, an apt metaphor for the war itself—hot with the temper of the opposing sides here, while over there, a war we could not win . . . we did not win. This now was the second in the new sequence of lost wars. Korea first, now Vietnam.

We all knew about the names before the memorial was announced and built. The names were important, their meaning being the only expressive measure in this war. The Vietnam Veterans Memorial honored the dead, the faceless dead. That was powerful!

When I received the Korean Wall Mural assignment, I knew immediately I'd have the Vietnam wall as a neighbor. And have it in comparison. How could I create another wall across the Reflecting Pool from this wall—one that would present a contrast to the wall of names, to its strength and its momentous success? The simplicity and directness of the Vietnam Memorial Wall vibrated for all who came . . . mothers, fathers, girlfriends, neighbors, schoolteachers. Babysitters. Shop keepers. Asians and Africans. Europeans, Latinos. On television, especially on the patriotic national holidays of Memorial Day, Veterans Day, Independence Day, there would be slow pans over the personal mementos being left—dog tags and photos, poems and handkerchiefs marked with a lipstick kiss. And in the news when the President recited the list of the wars, Vietnam would be readily included, and Korea at times forgotten. Where could my wall go? What was the meaning of a wall? Of this wall? Of their wall? What would it look like? Certainly, no use of names. Certainly not looking back in time and its shame.

∽✲∼

When the Vietnam Memorial Design Competition was announced in November 1980, twenty-one-year-old Maya Ying Lin was an architectural undergraduate student at Yale University and was fortunate to have dedicated instructors surrounding her. One of her professors, Andrus Burr, had recently shifted his course to deal with "funerary architecture." He integrated the competition into his course and encouraged Lin to enter her design. He helped resolve her design composed of two depressed triangular black granite walls of names. I credit Andrus Burr for his significant work in encouraging and doing all that good instructors do to encourage talent. Lin called it "a rift in the earth." In March 1981 the special jury of nine professionals in Washington, DC chose hers as the winning design from the 1,421 competitive entries.

I recall reading in the papers that two men—H. Ross Perot, the American business magnate who helped sponsor the design competition, and Jim Webb, the future senator from Virginia—withdrew their support for Lin's design; Webb called it "a nihilistic slab of granite" and Perot called it a "trench". Meanwhile James Watt, the Secretary of the Interior refused, at first, to award the memorial a building permit because of the public outcry. In spite of the strong objections from many sectors of the country and veterans—not all veterans—Lin's design would become highly successful; once the memorial was dedicated, people came. They came by the thousands, and many more thousands, veterans came . . . many wept in front of the black granite fonts—the names of their friends, of their family members—strangers and soldiers, brothers in arms. Families and friends came. Lin's design eventually prevailed against many strong conservative powers.

Names of the dead weren't enough. The controversy among Washington stalwarts over the wall's design was partly abated when Lin eventually agreed to the addition of Frederick Hart's sculptures of three male soldiers representing three cultures who fought in the war. (Hart coincidentally had come in third in the memorial design competition). Three standing male sculptures. A few years later another sculpture was added by Glenna Goodacre, showing a seated nurse holding a fallen injured soldier on her lap, attending to his wounds.

Lin strongly objected to these changes. After winning the competition, during the design process, she consulted with Kent Cooper and Bill Lecky, the memorial's Architects-of-Record. Ultimately, she supervised the development and details of the memorial, even with the additions and ideas that were not in her original design.

Every designer makes compromises in the design process—some call them adjustments. Internally, I ask myself, is it better this way or should I move this? The next day I could change it back. It's normal in the private process of creative decision-making. And also normal in the public process with staff and many times with a client.

Dedication day for the memorial came and Ronald Reagan attended the ceremony. At that ceremony, Maya Lin's name was omitted from the program. Again!

Since the Vietnam wall went up, hundreds, eventually tens of thousands, perhaps millions have come to seek the names of their comrades and their loved ones. Some with heads bowed and hands clasped together, as in prayer. Some with their heads against the wall and their forearms resting above, weeping, then walking away . . . only to return once more, in an hour, or a different day, to slowly trace the name with their finger, not wanting to leave.

Yet for many, in the memorial's simplicity something was missing. Regardless of the virtues of this fresh, simple design, in its original form, it was a partial memorial in that it remembered only the dead. The wounded and near dead were missing. And, it dismissed those who had returned and were ignored by a public who had rightly lost faith in their leaders and forgot those selected in the draft to fight the war who were also their brothers and sisters—Americans.

In the years following the completion of Hart's *Three Soldiers*, tributes to the Vietnam War seemed to proliferate, all in an attempt to recognize those left out of Lin's unprecedented design. Among Hart's sculpture of three soldiers and Glenna Goodacre's nurses and the flagstaff, there have been other additions and discussions of further add-ons, including a plaque commemorating veterans who died after the war, championed by Ruth Coder Fitzgerald; plans for an underground museum and a library of photos of those listed on the wall; and the ongoing incorporation of names missing from the original listing . . . how could that have happened?

The war and the Vietnam era were charged with emotional strife as we all started to realize the terrible loss of life and the reckless insanity and lies of our national leaders. We looked inward at ourselves and outward at our neighbors. The Wall and the mourning also left off the millions of Vietnamese who were slaughtered—their homes burned, their country blistered with bomb craters, their crops sprayed with Agent Orange. Should we honor those we saw as the enemy? Those who were the innocent citizens, not the Cong? It was unheard of to do so, un-American to think it could be done.

We grew emotionally as the demonstrations increased throughout the country and saw in horror the use of military force to quell protest on university campuses. We're reminded of the kneeling student crying in anguish over the body of a friend, shot dead at Kent State University. Shot by an American soldier. Arguably ordered by his American commanding officer.* At an American peace demonstration. On an American campus.

The country was waiting for a leader. One president decided not to re-run for the office, another resigned in disgrace. The populace who voted in decisive numbers for this individual was now disillusioned. They did not know their new leader, Gerald Ford. Decisions of previous administrations—from those of Eisenhower and his Domino Theory to those of Kennedy, Johnson and Nixon—were critically questioned. It would take years to heal.

The Vietnam Veterans Memorial and the furor surrounding it rekindled those terrible moments of hatred of the war and the abandonment of a president caught in his conspiracy against his own people. This memorial may have served its purpose regardless of its form and whether or not it had any figurative statues. However, it had survived. It had the proper balance of abstraction, purpose and timing.

In August 1995 I visited Vietnam with Judy for UNICEF. Two days were spent in the central highlands with the Muong ethnic minority living in stilt houses. While Judy was meeting with the women talking about the children and their care, I looked around the grouping of houses, took some photographs of the children smiling and dancing in front of my camera. I noticed a young girl with black hair, maybe nine or ten years old, coming from the

---

* "Although numerous investigatory commissions and court trials followed, during which members of the Ohio National Guard testified that they felt the need to discharge their weapons because they feared for their lives. However, disagreements remain as to whether they were, in fact, under sufficient threat to use force." https://www.history.com/topics/vietnam-war/kent-state-shooting

fields, quickly. She approached me and handed me a bunch of beautiful flowers she had just picked, her eyes filled with joy and her lips turned up into a smile... and she bowed. Much later I thought in shock of the anti-personnel land mines used throughout Vietnam, their maiming of civilian adults and children and the massive areas still contaminated after thirty years. A few days later, on the eve of their Constitutional holiday, the UNICEF group was walking in the center of Ho Chi Minh City from dinner back to our hotel, when another young child—this one no more than six (difficult to know age because of the years of malnutrition)—walked alongside of me and kept the back of his hand alongside of my left leg, faintly touching my trousers, not pressing but wanting to be attached, touching in a non-threatening way. After about twenty minutes, he disappeared. Our guide couldn't explain this, other than saying the boy liked me and trusted me and hoped I would take him away. These children knew little or nothing of the war. Their parents were infants or young adults twenty years before at the war's end. They all seemed gentle; we heard from the UNICEF staff that today's Vietnamese love Americans and hold no animosity against us for the war. A forgiving culture, although we were told that in the South, in the territory around the tunnels, this was not the case, that antipathy towards the Americans remained. We had, after all, destroyed their country, and it stood to reason that many felt the horror and shock and would continue to do so. Craters, the damage from Agent Orange, all would remain evidence of the American invaders.

Running one's hands over the engraved names at the Vietnam War Veterans Memorial, or over the faces of the Korean War Veterans Memorial mural brings a visitor into direct contact with the loss. It is said, you never own something unless you touch it. We learn this at both these memorials. Hands reaching out and touching the wall. Making a rubbing of the engraving is as natural today as it was with the floor slabs carved centuries ago in London's Westminster Abbey. By touching, we better understand not just the person we lost, but the ones who served, giving of their time and energy. By touching, we reacquaint ourselves with a loved one and the time we had with them. Touching enlivens our senses. I better comprehend what I missed and how I feel today... moved by this memorial through the act of being there, of reaching out to touch a name.

With its dedication in 1982, the Vietnam Veterans Memorial set a new standard for memorials, one not dependent on the stature of a leader but a recognition that a body of citizen soldiers paid for this war.

Korean Mural and Soldiers

Before the last flood washes over us
To leave us here on the sweet ground

EIGHT
CRISIS

A serious Crisis was about to happen. Before that, there was a Hitch. Frank Gaylord was well into his work on the sculptures when I decided to have portraits as the theme for the mural. We both were awaiting approval of the memorial's final design. The Commissions and the Advisory Board had yet to decide as the memorial was now in redesign because of conflicts with the original concept presented by BL3. So, the Hitch!

BL3—comprised of Veronica Burns Lucas, Don Alvaro Leon, John Paul Lucas, and Eliza Pennypacker Oberholtzer, landscape architecture instructors at Penn State University—was the winning design team for the memorial competition. But after evaluation by the architects-of-record and much discussion, their proposal could not be approved by the client group (the Advisory Board and the ABMC) and would have difficulties with the approving commissions—the Commission of Fine Arts and the National Capital Planning Commission. There were complications with the proposed siting. The footprint of the memorial was to be a semi-circular, half-moon with a double long line of thirty-eight sculptures; nineteen in each line in various ordered and disordered segments, symbolically depicting the evolving months of the war. The plan did not easily fit the site and might require removal of some large trees, however the main objection was to BL3's intention to minimize the interpretive specifics of the sculptural details on the statues. Their concept was an elusive, allegorical dream-like presence of ghostly figures moving across a remote landscape. The Advisory Board did not understand this initial concept, believing the sculptures should provide a realistic line of soldiers—trusting that realism in the details and equipment on the statues would help tell the story of a brutal and bloody war.

General Raymond Davis, foreman of the jury, in describing the BL3 concept, commented, "To us, it was very realistic, and we were kind of surprised at all the symbolism the designers had in mind. They saw figures as a passage of time, where we saw a combat formation." BL3 conceived the sculptures to be carved in granite, but the details that the Advisory Board requested would require casting in metal. Initially hired as consultants to the architect-of-record, BL3 did not want to make the recommended changes in the statues and the layout. They filed a lawsuit against the Advisory Board, Army Corps of Engineers, American Battle Monuments Commission, Cooper-Lecky, and the design competition organization, eventually losing their case. They were then fired by the Advisory Board and relieved of any further involvement with the project.

Cooper-Lecky was asked to re-plan the concept and if approved would also then become the design architects. Lecky asked me to meet with him in Washington to review the new directions for the memorial's layout. It was very different from BL3's plan that showed a field of thirty-eight troops in two lines of nineteen soldiers crossing a seemingly separate wall having no specified subject or function. Cooper-Lecky's revised memorial was now shown as a triangular field, which they called "The Field of Service." Within the field would be a dispersed combat ready column of thirty-eight soldiers, flanked by a long granite wall composed of my portrait concept. The sculptures would be reflected on the smooth polished wall mural surface. They would be heading toward a circular pool of running water, called the "Pool of Remembrance" in dedication to those soldiers who had fallen. It looked good and now seemed to have a structure that fit the site. In particular, the mural wall would be integrated into the composition and not detached. I liked it. We discussed a number of my thoughts regarding the mural wall, its height and the slope of the land, and some details in the wall structure that would help the mural design, specifically the joinery of the panels as I wanted my images to easily flow from panel to panel forming a continuous 164-foot long uninterrupted mural.

Kent Cooper and Bill Lecky skillfully managed the project through the early difficult stages of obtaining clarity in the faulty competition-winning design, and through the redesign, merging the fountain and lighting plans with Frank Gaylord's soldiers and my mural. Along the way, they undertook numerous meetings, giving presentations to the Advisory Board, the Commission of Fine Arts, the National Capital Planning Commission and other government organizations.

Early in the project, on the approval of the Advisory Board, the architects-of-record had selected Frank Gaylord to create the composition of infantry. Serious, stoic yet kindly, Gaylord was a sculptor who lived in Barre, Vermont. He had solid experience in regional figurative stone sculpture; he had also served in WWII with the 17th Airborne Division and was awarded the Bronze Star for his service. He presented his concept of the sculptures to the commission—thirty-eight carved granite statues of foot soldiers in Korea, including Air Force and Navy liaison. Each would be slightly taller than life-size, showing details of the uniform and weapons. It was an extraordinary composition and would be a challenge to complete in stone because of those details.

Time constraints, fine points of the uniforms and equipment, and long-term maintenance dictated casting the sculptures in stainless steel instead of stone. Additionally, physically cutting and sculpting thirty-eight sculptures in the remaining 4 years to meet a dedication date would present another problem. As the overall memorial design went through the various stages of the approval process, the number of the soldiers was also revised—reduced from thirty-eight to nineteen. The Advisory Board thought that thirty-eight soldiers in this triangular space would create an unrealistic concentration for a battle-ready unit. In actual combat, the soldiers were too close to each other—suggesting vulnerability to enemy fire. Apparently, the National Capital Planning Commission voiced similar concerns. They also reasoned the reduction to nineteen sculptures could still retain the symbolic, yet illusory need of thirty-eight with their reflections in the adjacent polished granite wall. I personally doubt the visitor would see this however it might serve as a talking point by the docents.

Frank Gaylord and I always got along very well; I cannot recall us ever having a disagreement. Before we had even met, we were in close contact regardless of the distance between my office in Manhattan and his studio in Barre. We met in person at a team meeting in the architect's office in Cambridge and again at his studio. With my lead designer, I flew to Burlington, rented a car and drove on Interstate 89 through the Green Mountains to Barre. Snow was falling so fast on portions of the two-hour ride that I had a challenge holding the rental to the slippery roads. In Barre, a granite town of mills, I easily located Frank's studio, a 5,500 square-foot shed with a weathered exterior, built of heavy timbers with a thirty-foot-high ceiling. He greeted me in the doorway of the standard-size entrance next to enormous sliding doors built to move large pieces in and out of his workspace. Inside, we walked under a twenty-ton overhead crane on a steel track. I gazed up at its height and might in wonder. The floor and surfaces, Frank told me, would usually be covered with light grey stone dust, freshly swept clean for my visit—today my black clothes were reasonably safe!

Frank's drawings were pinned on some of the walls and parts of previous sculptures placed in the dark recesses; maquettes of the nineteen soldiers he was working on were the center attraction. I had not seen them in the flesh before and was awed by their power and impressed with Frank, his calm presence, his amazing work—his space—an ideal place for this artist's work on our shared design of the Korean Veteran's Memorial.

The architects Kent Cooper and Bill Lecky soon arrived, having also braved the drive through the storm. I could see they too were impressed with the studio and of course with Frank's work on the soldier's statues—the maquettes. I had brought a number of scaled mural elevations to place alongside Frank's arrangement of maquettes on a twenty-foot long table. (Cooper-Lecky had a similar table built in an annex of their Washington office to facilitate reviews and presentations.) We viewed the mock-ups, made notes, commented, discussed . . . not many long discussions with Frank at the meeting. Frank was a man of few words as he sketched some details between us and nodded, yes. I knew we were on the same wavelength and the same path.

Back in New York I thought over what I had learned about the size of the portraits, from seeing Frank's sculptures grouped with my images of the wall mural. Re-worked, refined, I made more mock-ups, and went again to Barre in a few weeks. A number of the portraits were rendered full-size, so that we could see how the visitor would be able to look eye-to-eye with the soldiers of 1950, see themselves reflected in the polished granite together with the soldiers, who were looking out at Frank's sculptures and at their future, full of hope. My team photographed the mock-ups and projected the slides full-size to get a real-life sense of the memorial, and to use for presentations in Washington.

Getting the portrait images into the granite didn't seem like a problem. In fact, the granite turned out to be much easier to work than I had initially expected. However it required the skills from a number of technologically trained artists, some with digital backgrounds and others with an acute understanding of stone and big, heavy machines and still others who possessed the ability to calculate the different grit powder sizes and pressure volumes of air blasts needed to "engrave" dots at certain depths in a granite surface. With the expert team from Coldspring granite, whom we had hired to manufacture the panels, we were able to apply this state-of-the-art technology to create the mural.

Early in the process, I had reasoned, if a series of dots could be printed in ink to produce a photograph in a newspaper, a series of dots could be "sandblasted" into granite to produce a photograph in stone. That's an oversimplification, but basically it was the concept of the transfer of photographic "halftone" images from the light-sensitive print mask to the hard-granular polished stone. Seems obvious and simple today. Yet, in between there were many steps utilizing highly accurate computer technology and making painstaking adjustments to the quality-controlled photosensitive, grit-resistive rubberized masks holding the "dot" patterns, all performed by this small group of talented artisans proficient in modern and ancient techniques. Jennifer coordinated much of the details of the final design and technological coordination, passing key items to me for approval.

I asked Coldspring's team to produce a number of samples showing the variety of sizes of the "mezzotint dots" and the depth of the engraved "sandblasted" image. This variety was honed toward finding the optimum solution. Constant refinements adjusted the "mezzotint" to carefully relate to the granular structure of the granite.

The mezzotint—an older term for an intaglio or engraved image printing process—is, in other words, an irregular custom shaped dot or spot that can appear similar to the granular structure of granite. We wanted this "shaped dot" to coordinate with the granular structure of the granite, so that when one looked at the mural at an arm's length, the faces would appear to belong to the granite—growing out of it, one might say, and not merely applied to the surface by a series of circular dots.

My team tested these patterns—composed portraits, some larger, some smaller, some with a deep cut blast, others softer or not so deep—all on two-foot square, one-inch thick granite panels. We tested a white compound-fill to see if that enhanced the images. It looked false. Also, we tested a waterproof compound to coat the mural images so that the portraits would not disappear in a heavy rain or light drizzle. That worked. We decided to use the compound, as the dry time of the wet granite took too long to reveal the faces, denying the visitors a viewing experience. Moreover, a rainy day with a north wind might render the mural unseeable until the rain or the wind stopped.

Innumerable samples were made by Coldspring to our specifications and sent to my office in New York. Each was carefully packed and encased in a wooden crate. They would arrive every few weeks on an 18-wheeler flatbed, creating traffic tie-ups on my street, University Place, and delays in the narrow streets of Greenwich Village in Manhattan, New York City. A similar delivery would be made to Cooper-Lecky's offices in the Georgetown neighborhood of Washington, DC.

We would review the pieces in our office, set them against the wall on the sidewalk outdoors facing north, the direction the mural would face in Washington, so we could see how the sun would affect the quality of the portraits. And observe the effect of a cloudy day. At times, the crated samples showed variances in the contrast of the image in the stone resulting from different grit blast depths and powder density, each variance grit blasted to our specification and marked on the reverse side of the sample. Between Cooper-Lecky and us, we would deliberate, make telephone calls, live with the samples overnight and make the calls again. In some cases, we would wait a few days in order to get a fresh look.

Finally, all the pieces were brought together in a scale model set up in Washington, DC, at Cooper-Lecky's annex, nineteen scaled sculptures (maquettes) in combat gear armed with rifles, some slung and some at the ready, trudging up a shallow hill past the mural. Here, we made further adjustments. Meanwhile, the team gave myriad presentations to the Advisory Board, and conducted informal and formal showings to Carter Brown and the Fine Arts Commission.

Little did we know, the crisis was about to happen. It was June 8, 1991 and Washington had just celebrated General Schwarzkopf's Gulf War victory on the National Mall, and a victorious ticker-tape parade in New York City. As was explained to me by Bill Lecky, and to him by the secretary of the Fine Arts

Commission, the citizens of Washington were shocked by the public show of the nation's military might on display on the National Mall—tanks and armored personnel carriers, machine guns, helicopters and artillery pieces and rifles. It was explained by the secretary that people were not comfortable seeing guns and rifles in the open in the Nation's Capital. This discomfort may affect the approval of our concept of the memorial by the Fine Arts Commission. I was told, because Frank's stainless-steel soldiers were visibly carrying rifles, the Commission was on the cusp of disapproving our design.

Hearing this, I instinctively knew we must cover the guns. Simple. Others were walking around with long gloomy faces. I suggested to the architects and Frank that the soldiers could wear ponchos. They would not only cover the rifles, but also—if they were shown as if rippling in the breeze—create a lyrical flow of air between the soldiers, unifying and further strengthening the nineteen. Cooper nodded and Frank agreed. Within a short time, he was able to adjust his maquettes. Everyone was pleased with the results. The Fine Arts Commission agreed to this change. There were more steps to take, but for now our design was saved. The crisis disappeared.

I've lost count of the trips made to Cold Spring, Minnesota, where the granite was cut to size and each of the mural's panels were being carefully grit blasted by the craftsmen, working in a closed-off section of the enormous production floor. We would discuss details and procedures at length, select the exact type of granite—dark grey Academy Black—and review the variances in color and grain that we could expect. Our work would be done in a series of gigantic sheds, hot in the summer and freezing cold, even with heaters, in the winter as the wind would find its way around the inside of my hard-hat, which ably provided protection to my head from bumps but not from frost, even when wearing a knitted scull-cap. The factory's steel structure was a football field in length and easily 40-50 feet in height, emitting a loud constant din from the cutting machines and cranes moving gigantic pieces of stone; a noise so loud that at the end of just four hours, I would feel a dramatic sense of fatigue.

Cold Spring, Minnesota, is about an hour and half drive from the airport in Minneapolis. This is Garrison Keillor country and I would often laugh thinking of his remarks, on the radio the previous Saturday night's Prairie Home Companion, about Lake Wobegon, somewhere west of Interstate I-94 as I would drive to Cold Spring. Minneapolis and St. Paul were where my stepson Clark lived with his wife, Alyson and daughter, Hollis. These trips would become more difficult after January 1992.

All designers of the National Mall sites have worked with care and dedication to bring their work to the nation, as I have. Each occupied according to their own careful timetable as I was working according to mine. (As it turns out there will not be many others after me, as the Memorial Commission has now restricted any further memorials from being placed on the Mall.) During one of my trips to Coldspring granite, I saw massive dark gray granite stones being assembled into a tall wall. They told me this was a mock-up for Lawrence Halprin's FDR Memorial. Striking in its simplicity, these rectangular cut stones, easily three by five feet by two or more feet deep, some larger, sitting atop one another, rising to fifteen feet or more. Massive. A few years would go by before I'd see them again in Washington, in their place at the Franklin Delano Roosevelt Memorial on the Mall. Halprin died in 2009 at the age of ninety-three, twelve years after this work was completed. Halprin started work on the memorial in 1974. He endured a delay of twenty years before Congress provided funds to continue and finish the design work. I can only imagine how proud he must have been to see his memorial realized, after so many years.

⁂

The Fine Arts Commission was to have a final review of our work on Thursday, January 16, 1992. Most of the critical design work had been completed. Judy and I cut short our normal early January vacation and flew back from the sun and warmth of the Caribbean to New York. On Wednesday, the 15th, I flew to Washington, DC, checked into the Four Seasons Hotel in Georgetown, close to Cooper-Lecky's offices. At 8 p.m. that night, I received a call from my brother-in-law, Denver, telling me, in barely audible words, "Clark had taken his life."

My heart fell. I wanted to talk with Judy. I needed to talk to her. Denver said she was devastated and couldn't speak. We spoke further, somehow or other, made plans to meet at the airport in Minneapolis, the following afternoon. I hung up. My mind was a blank. I felt cold. We knew Clark had been suffering and was in a great deal of pain about his disintegrating marriage and losing his sobriety. Oh Judy! How could she bear this? I have no idea how all the arrangements for my flight and hotels in Saint Paul were made. Thankful for both the staffs of my and Judy's offices. The following morning, I woke exhausted, gathered things together, checked out of the Four Seasons, caught a cab, got to the presentation and listened silently as Cooper and Lecky made the presentation to Fine Arts. Carter Brown and the Commission gave our team the final approval of our design of the Memorial. It was a bittersweet triumph. Earlier that morning, I told Bill Lecky what had happened. After the meeting, he drove me to National Airport. When I got out of his car, I turned and nodded my thanks and congratulated him on our approval ... shook my head sadly and walked away when I should have been skipping with joy. The start of a long process of grieving and healing overpowered any celebration of our Fine Arts approval.

The suicide of her son could, I knew, could have broken Judy, as it has so many others. But it didn't. Her strength and her program prevailed. She lived through the time, as others have—as I have. It was terrible but we did the work required, the therapy, the grief counseling. The talking. It would take a number of years for Judy and me to design and build a memorial to Clark, and a few years to finish building the Korean War Veterans Memorial. As you might expect, the two live in my mind and Judy's for all these years, hand in hand one might say. Each visit to Washington DC, I stop at the Korean memorial and think of Clark. And there still isn't a time when visiting Minneapolis/Saint Paul is easy.

Weeks later, back in the studio, with the Fine Arts approval, my team and I proceeded to bring the selection of portraits to a close. We determined their final sizes—some full-size, others smaller—and retouched them as necessary; in some cases, shifting the illumination from the left side to right side of the portrait so that everyone would be illuminated by the morning sun coming from the east. We then processed each into reproduction mezzotint prints, all to be pasted onto "mechanical" 30 x 40-inch boards as the finished design. It took months to complete. Afterward, each panel would be photographed full-size, transmitted to Coldspring granite for the final production to our specification. More than two thousand portraits—the full selection for the forty-one panels that the architects and the Advisory Board would inspect and approve. My team did an unbelievable job, the scope and complexity of which had never previously been accomplished.

Tomb of the Unknown Soldier

Once more join together to celebrate and
Remember all that could have been
Remember all that could have been

NINE
A JUST WAR?

On a visit to the memorial, retired Navy surgeon Bill Lascheid stood in front of the mural with his wife, Nancy, and named each member of his surgical team, one-by-one, as he remembered them many years ago, all working under his surgical tent in Korea with shells erupting and the lights dimming. Naming each nurse. Each doctor. Standing there, he once again gave them thanks.

Look at the wall, and you may see Navy surgeon Bill Lascheid who jumped into a bunker to give aide to a fallen Marine. Look again and you may see Bill Weber, the badly wounded commander of an airborne infantry company. Look deeper and see his hope. When we speak of the Korean War Veterans Memorial, some may remember a forgotten cold and bloody war lost in the confusion at the end of an era morphing into the fear of an uncertain Cold War. Others may envision a group of statues and a mass of portraits, the faces of lost years as our youth served us all. Look again, and you might see John Phillips who served near Old Baldy.

Portrait likenesses have commemorated those who have been important to us by countless methods and in untold places, from the deep bronze reliefs on the doors of the baptistery of the Duomo in Florence; to the bas-relief of Civil War soldiers on the march in Washington, DC and another on the Boston Commons; to the images of patrons in paintings by Rembrandt and in stained glass in the world's cathedrals.

Images on graves have marked the site of those departed from the earliest of times to the present, as can be seen in the low reliefs on Egyptian stone walls and the deep bas-reliefs used in ancient Rome, to the clear plastic-covered photos on grave markers in Central Europe during the middle of the last century. In this century, photographs of our proud youth, now dead in Iraq and Afghanistan, have been displayed in a scrolling honor roll on the PBS NewsHour. Watching their faces, reading their names, hometowns, branches of service, and ranks night after night, I tremble at the absurdity of this needless loss.

Life and living prevail in the midst of the wars. Feelings of the day weave a course between individuals and families. By the sixteenth century, Shakespeare wrote of rival families in Verona—the Capulets and the Montagues—and told the ritual of hate within the tragic love story of Romeo and Juliet; Rodgers and Hammerstein wrote, "The Farmer and the Cowman should be friends" for *Oklahoma!;* and Arthur Laurents penned (with lyrics by Stephen Sondheim and music by Leonard Bernstein) a modern-day tale of the Capulets and Montagues in New York's *West Side Story.*

People love war stories, even as they hate living through times of conflict. Those stories do not change. Humanity continues to be comprised of warriors, aggressors, defenders and survivors—the innocent and the guilty. Ironically, we continue to wage wars with the full knowledge that, as Richard Holbrooke—the veteran U.S. diplomat—said, "eventually the war will end, and people will sit at a negotiating table."

In time, civility tempered the killing of the losing leader, mitigated at times by retaining hostages to be released with payments of money, land, ransoms of other redemptions, or even rehabilitation, many in answer to family appeals or greater needs. (Within our own time, the Marshall Plan, created after WWII, was a massive economic recovery program to aid both the rebuilding of the cities of Europe and the people devastated during that war, while starting to stabilize a world order . . . for the common good of all.) Yet killing persists. Historically, international accords have prevailed with formal conventions, for example: the Geneva Conventions of 1864, 1929 and 1949 with additional protocols establishing standards for humane treatment during war, and the Treaty of Versailles after World War I. The first Hague Peace Conference, convened in 1899 by Tsar Nicholas of Russia, had the purpose of addressing "rules of war." Trials would be set up to prosecute the guilty of war crimes; consider those that took place at Nuremberg, Germany, in 1945-6, and at the 2006 Hague International Court of Justice regarding genocide in Bosnia. The guilty would be judged. Reparations would be levied.

A JUST WAR? 133

But not in the case of Bosnia. "... financial compensation for the failure to prevent the genocide at Srebrenica was not the appropriate form of reparation. The Court considered that the most appropriate form of satisfaction would be a declaration...that Serbia had failed to comply with the obligation to prevent the crime of genocide... that Serbia had violated its obligations under the Convention and that it must transfer individuals accused of genocide to the ICTY and must co-operate fully with the Tribunal..."

Wars, great or small are borne by soldiers, sailors and flyers, all made vital by their moment in battle, for they are the ones who make great the war. Their leaders composed the strategy. Yet, the energy and the story come from the front line, the "grunts" who face the trouble, day or night in searing heat or breath-taking freezing cold. At the onset, I asked, could my mural serve a larger purpose than what I was asked to create? Could the mural I envisioned also serve as a broader national statement—not only to those who had fought in Korea but for those who fight in all wars. After all, the common denominator for all those wars, present and past, are the soldiers. Might this mural define how a nation commemorates service? Could my mural add to the presence of the Lincoln and Vietnam memorials? Will each of them be better for what I bring to the Korean Memorial?

One evening at a dinner party, hoping for a fresh view of war, I asked my dinner companion about the human condition in relation to our preference to solve differing issues with neighbors by violence. He said, "Well, there's Cain and Abel."

Did it start there, I asked? Did it start with Abel's murder and Cain's negotiation with God?

The following morning, I went to Genesis in the Bible. I had read it a very long time ago. I read it again. And then again. And again. It's a very short story, merely sixteen verses. I searched interpretive books and articles about Abel and Cain, talked with Jim Kowalski, the new dean at the Cathedral of Saint John the Divine. I dug further into the ways in which others attempted to resolve conflict. To be sure, the Korean Veterans memorial is about the men and women. But it is also about a war, and about all those caught in that war and, for that matter all wars, and in some manner about the "moral authority" of their leaders.

Eons after the scribes of the Bible wrote the story of Cain and Abel, the Roman Emperor Constantine I sought to reconcile strong differences within the church and its external affairs. In 325 AD, he instituted an ecumenical conference, the First Council of Nicaea, fostering the settlement of conflicts through negotiation and compromise, resulting in worldwide agreements among the disciples of Christ. They established the Nicene Creed, a set of beliefs that reconciled schisms, disagreements about the Father and the Son, other doctrine, standards and practices as it established a uniform ecclesiastical calendar. There were times in the coming centuries when the Creed, or at least the ideas behind it, seemed to clear the path for humane behavior in wartime—at least for those who believed in Christ. And many today recite the Nicene Creed each Sunday.

The Catholic Church, first through St. Augustine of Hippo (354–430) and later St. Thomas Aquinas (1225–1274), justified the use of force in the service of God with proclamations on "Just Wars." The reader might be interested to see how various "schools" and individuals have revised their arguments, over time, for the sake of humanity, i.e., restoring "good" by any means to achieve a swift and complete victory over the enemy. Again, a swift and complete victory.

In the seventh century, the 1st Caliph, Abu Bakr, gave his Muslim army ten rules. They included instructions to his soldiers not to mutilate the dead, nor kill children, women or aged men; not to destroy trees or the enemy's flock; and to leave the enemy's monastic peoples alone. These stipulations might lose their power in the coming centuries, but the humanity of those rules is striking—a sign of compassion in the midst of the clash of armies, night or day.

Still, violence continued to be the watchword of the times. What were these quests about: power or religion . . . or something else? In 1095, Pope Urban II encouraged the first Crusades in an effort to wrest Jerusalem from the Turks, who had launched successful raids on Christian footholds in the Middle Eastern countries. Financial and spiritual support for these Crusades came from a series of Popes and Knights. Sigurd I of Norway was the first European King to undertake a Crusade in 1107. Forty years later, in 1147, Eleanor of Aquitaine, the Queen of France, went on the Second Crusade. Married to Louis VII, and twenty-five years old, she led three hundred vassals from her Duchy and dozens of her ladies-in-waiting onto the fields of battle, determined to attend to the wounded. Witnesses reported that an abundance of luggage and jewels accompanied the young Queen. She lived well and traveled well. The Lady ventured into the far reaches of Constantinople and Antioch in her quest. In spite of the humanitarian efforts of Eleanor and her ladies, the armies of Germany and France, with whom Eleanor was traveling, were roundly defeated by the Seljuk Turks, and the Second Crusade was deemed a failure. Eleanor's presence on the Crusade broke an unwritten rule of the times. Thereafter, a papal bull was issued, expressly forbidding women to join the next Crusade. It would remain in effect for the next three centuries.

Richard the Lionheart, Eleanor's son born during her second marriage to King Henry II of England, was crowned in 1189. He immediately led the Third Crusade to free Jerusalem from the armies of Saladin, a Sunni Muslim, the first sultan of Egypt and Syria and founder of the Ayyubid dynasty. Richard raised money for his Turkish Wars by selling many of his royal mansions and castles and was quoted as saying that if he could, he would have "sold London itself." In the duels between their armies, both Richard and Saladin beheaded the vanquished by the hundreds, perhaps more. Yet, a history of the Third Crusade by James Reston, Jr. seems to paint Saladin more tolerant than Richard, at least to me. Still, horror runs through war, almost by definition.

It is reasonable to suppose Richard was also thinking that he would redeem his mother's attempts to regain the Holy City. Still, his efforts ended much the same as his mother's, in failure to recapture Jerusalem. On Richard's return from the Third Crusade after the many years he spent in pursuit of victory over Saladin, he was captured by Leopold V, Duke of Austria—whom he had offended in Acre on the shores of the Mediterranean, in the Dominions of Saladin. He was kept in captivity for ransom. Richard was finally released, after his mother, Eleanor, had worked hard to raise the ransom for her son's freedom.

General Tecumseh Sherman may have been thinking of these histories during his rampage through Georgia, telling General Ulysses S. Grant he would "make Georgia howl." Sherman murdered, destroyed and burned every inch of Georgia's ground as he plowed through the state with his Union Army. We know these stories shift from side to side. A noted historian once told me Sherman did not burn and pillage as he has been accused. Yet, as with Richard and Saladin, Sherman may have truly forged a path of destruction, a scorched-earth policy in action. However, in various readings, there is little difference between a medieval beheading and the American Civil War horrors at Andersonville.

The Crusades went on through the reigns of Pope Gregory IX and the Sixth Crusade (1228–1229), the Seventh and the Knights Templar, and beyond to the Ninth Crusade in 1271. All this violence was waged in hopes of wresting the holy city of Jerusalem as well the Holy Land from the dominion of Byzantium, the Turks and Muslims. All these stories tell of the leader, the King of the era and the leader of the battle. They, and their scribes mostly lived to tell the tale … it was their men who died by the thousands.

*

The author David Halberstam reflects on the differences between the fifties and the sixties, between Korea and Vietnam in relation to the United States, a country once a democracy turned empire, as he put it in *The Next Century*. His words seem so fitting when I see the two memorial walls, Korea and Vietnam. One, so moving yet so impersonal in its long, long list of names, showing loss, reflecting the dispassionate commitment of a group of men—a President, a General, a Cabinet Secretary—furthering their own needs for which America's youth paid. The other, composed of faces of yesterday and conveys the reasoned, heartbreaking commitment of the leaders and the men and women who served in a conflict too quickly forgotten at a time of migrating ethical standards—and yet a long way off from being settled.

It's not a leap to see how bullying with fights of words, tweets or fists is a natural extension of our need to go to war.

Why not settle the war and formalize a peace to the 1953 hostilities with an open door to a better understanding between the North and South, between the UN, USA and China, today? So suggests my friend, Jim Mitchell, in a *New York Times* letter to the editor on September 6, 2017. After all, wasn't it the North who within months of starting the Korea War, opened the discussions of a ceasefire? Jim envisions a resolution where all parties gain a common respect for one another and all leave winning. I have thought similarly, and I know many have agreed. Others believe in taking stock of the strengths and weaknesses of each and negotiate from that position. Another view comes from the former Secretary of State Henry Kissinger, who has suggested sending a distinguished emissary to China with our thoughts of the evolution of the region and initiate a broad discussion among Beijing, Seoul and Tokyo as to the steps that might be taken that could lead to peace in Korea and the region.

As bad as we believe things have become, "Steven Pinker has documented, we've seen a steady decline in wars and armed conflict," reports David Brooks in his *New York Times* column of October 16, 2017. This reminded me of Mr. Pinker's March 2007 TED Talk. In nineteen minutes, he quite carefully documented the surprisingly steady decline of hostilities from the age of the caveman to modern times, detailing a number of reasons. He emphasized an expansion of the logic of the Golden Rule, "Do unto others as you would have them do unto you," coupled with periods of travel, literacy and increased "cosmopolitan" knowledge of each opposing side, plus the applied pros and cons of preventive strikes—moving in another way of Richard Holbrooke's settling the conflict at the negotiating table before the war starts. Pinker asserted, "Today we are probably living in the most peaceful time in our species' existence." I wonder if that is true, as it seems to me that war is everywhere now—but Pinker ended his talk by saying if we ask, "Why is there war?" we should also ask, "Why is there peace?"

I worked hard during those five years of design and construction. Generally, slept well; although a few times in the early months, I would be somewhat restless, waking in the middle of the night, particularly when I was uncertain about the arrangement of the portraits. In the first weeks, I stirred at times with faces in my vision. Eyes, pairs of eyes staring into me. Yet, there was never a doubt about my path and where I was headed, supported always with an underlying sense that all would go well and the job would properly honor the men and women who served, as well as those who would come to remember and heal. I vividly recall the feeling of wonder throughout the design process of the mural—and occasionally, a dread, probably more a sense of anxiety.

It happened that way with most of my projects—a tiny degree of unsureness followed by a sense of confidence that would see me through. If I keep within my process and spend time on the details when they need to be worked on, not attend to them in the early months when I'm defining the overall concept, all will stay on track. As the design grew more defined, I sensed I was a conduit for the spirit to work through me and create a place for millions to spend a moment of time in their days and for the ages to come.

The contrasts between then and now, nearly seventy years later, sharpened. Because of the Memorial, it brought light to those who remember and lived through that time. The struggle of individuals in the heat of conflict during the cold Korean winters of the 1950s stands in stark relief to the struggles of today to strengthen the defense of the United States from seen and concealed aggression while assuring the safety of the free world. Perhaps in experiencing this memorial, we can start to fathom the innocence we lost on 9/11. Perhaps with the passing of time, and with a fresh understanding in resolving today's differences, we might arrive at agreements that bypass the taking of lives. Some ask, "Have we as a people learned to solve our conflicts and help our neighbors in solving theirs? Have we learned to understand ourselves and how so many have innocently been placed in harm's way?" In the end I realize that these three war-veteran memorials, Vietnam, Korea, and World War II, and the four presidential memorials, Washington, Lincoln, Jefferson and FDR, cannot be thought of as separate works. They stand together, reliant on one another. They reflect the leaders and the people, the dead and the time. They represent the burden of decisions and the responsiveness of youth, forever linked to us today as we honor them with each visit.

I read about the parasitic worms found in the stomach of a North Korean soldier, who had been shot and wounded fleeing across the 38th parallel in November 2017. Realizing this affliction must exist in much of North Korea's population—apparently due to the North's using human refuse for fertilizer—it seems another sensible decision would be for us to help North Korea to provide better nutrition and health for their people, while assuring them of our support for their national and regional security—all as a deterrent to their further development and use of nuclear weapons—a first of many steps to normalization in the region.

Permanence, in this transitory time, is an odd concept. Before receiving the Korean War Veterans Memorial Mural commission, I had yearned for a project whose realization would endure forever. Up to that time, most of my projects would last a few years, or perhaps a decade, whether an interior, exhibition or a product. I designed this memorial with the hope that future generations will view the faces on the wall with a sense of familiarity; that the faces will remind them of their own time, of those that look out from across the dining room table or their bathroom mirror every morning, or from their television or newspaper in relation to yet other wars—just as the faces in the Civil War photos had reminded me of soldiers in other wars. Eyes tell a universal story, particularly when surrounded with the greyness of hostilities.

This all may be hopeful, for what we mostly experience, is the past forever holding us back with the old habits and frailties of Cain seeking to live without the mark. Or, perhaps Cain still believing the mark protects him. The story reverberates with twists and turns, as with Lady Macbeth, who cries, "Out, damned spot." In another long step of history, the Soviet Union disintegrates from its world presence as it suffered the cost of Afghanistan and its own internal battles. America followed the Soviet Union into Afghanistan, as the Red Army leaves the mountains and returns to their bankrupted country—similarly as the United States followed the French into Vietnam, as did the Chinese and the Japanese, before. Sometime after Vietnam, did we finally learn that we could not afford the battles and the arms and the technology—while maintaining the advanced standard-of-living that we in America had grown accustomed? Even so, we supported a war in Iraq and Afghanistan, without some form of sacrifice in our standard of living—as we sacrificed foods and supplies during World War II. We abandoned selecting who fights the war when the draft was terminated in January 1973, shifting the war's emotional toll onto a volunteer Army; in the process, distancing the citizens from decisions about where and why their children are sent into battle.

The Greeks believed that a cathartic release experienced in their dramas reduced the public's need to act out their violence in real life. The Olympics mirrored that philosophy. Yet the Greeks propagated the Peloponnesian War and the battles between their city-states. The theater has clearly not fully quelled the need for arms, or armies, or battles. Today, real life violence by individuals, driven by their own voices and visions, kills innocents in Columbine and Aurora, Colorado and on the campus in Virginia and Texas and a school in Connecticut. Violence and shootings in Charlotte and Charleston. Innocents are killed just as readily as those killed in Korea, Vietnam, Iraq or Afghanistan, in war or in the security of peace at home . . . using the same weapons in both places.

A child psychiatrist friend tells me she is increasingly concerned with bullying amongst the youth in her community and within her practice. It's not a leap to see how intimidating with force of words, tweets or fists is a natural extension of a need to go to war.

It would seem sitting at Holbrook's negotiating table before the maiming and destruction would be sensible, whether the war is between peoples on opposite sides, or the war between the opposite sides in one's own head. Doesn't it make sense! People, seemingly sane, statesmen or factory workers, men or women, finally, must sit there, and for as long as it takes. After the deaths, after the maiming, the returning veterans, the strife within the citizens, the war crime trials, the negotiation within one's self . . . life is reconstructed while death is memorialized. How to get all the actors to the table? All!

In July 1994, I accompanied Judy, who also is a UNICEF Goodwill Ambassador and International Representative for the Arts, to Bosnia and Herzegovina. In Mostar, we saw the remains of a bombed city, the demolished Stari Most Bridge that crossed the Neretva River connecting two different cultures of the city, two ethnic groups who had once lived, worked and socialized in peace, but now no longer talk with each other. We saw the drawings of children distressed by war. We walked in the streets with the school kids singing—a few running ahead of Judy to stop her, saying, "This is where the snipers get you." We met the schoolmaster who had to gingerly walk an unstable rope bridge across the river Neretva to attend to the Muslim children's education. We saw classrooms in the cellars where school was held; all while hearing shelling from the mountains in our view. Before the war, the children from all the districts would attend school together. Now they're separated. They spoke the same language; now they only talk their own languages. Later, at a meeting with the town leaders—the three mayors, each from the Bosnian, Croat and Serb communities, and a fourth mayor, the EU-appointed leader and arbiter (whose life had but a few weeks before been threatened by one of the other mayors)—Judy presented what she learned about the children and how they have been traumatized by the war and the tenuous peace. The four men stared at her with incredulous expressions on their faces, as if they had no idea how this war was affecting their own children and their future.

A JUST WAR?

Twice a year we honor our veterans. On Memorial Day and Veterans Day, each anchored by a significant war. On those days, veterans of all ages gather in groups, many in uniform, some wearing hats of the American Legion or the Veterans of Foreign Wars (VFW).

Memorial Day was originally observed as Decoration Day, honoring the nation's dead that the North and the South suffered during the Civil War. The dead were remembered in cemeteries and city parks after 1865. Its name gradually changed to Memorial Day, first used in 1882 and finally changed in 1967, celebrated at the end of May in observance of all veterans, all wars.

In many communities, local military academies march to the beat of their bands; veterans ride motorcycles through the streets to remember those missing in action. Elsewhere naval ships dock at the piers while sailors celebrate in Times Square; jets put on air shows for the people picnicking below; and stands are filled for ball games in the parks, everyone hoping the sun will shine and it will not rain.

Veterans Day—once called Armistice Day—initiated after World War I, The Great War, proclaimed by President Woodrow Wilson on November 11, 1919. In 1918, hostilities ended at the 11th hour on the 11th day of the 11th month. In the United States, red poppies, represented in John McCrae's poem, "In Flanders Fields," were distributed by the Veterans of Foreign Wars. In Commonwealth nations (United Kingdom, Canada, Australia, India, South Africa, Singapore and others, totaling fifty-three independent member states), the day is still called Remembrance Day. In 1954, President Eisenhower and Congress changed Armistice Day to Veterans Day, to remember the veterans of all wars, World War I, World War II, including the recently returned soldiers and officers of the Korean War. (I still like the title Armistice Day, remembering this older tradition as applied to our modern time.)

World War II veterans came back from The Good War to celebrations on Main Street of their victories in Europe and the Pacific. They seldom shared their stories and left them for others to tell in film and music and books: Richard Rodgers's *Victory at Sea* and Tom Brokaw's *The Greatest Generation*—separated by decades. Millions of brothers and sisters were left in cemeteries throughout Europe and the Pacific. Those who returned went directly to work (many went directly to school) as the nation grew in an expanding economy, to realize a better quality of life for their families. Many still could not talk about their war experiences. Fear, perhaps terror of the memories, kept their secrets of the horrors locked tightly in their hearts and minds. They would have to wait decades to see their recognition in the World War II Memorial on the National Mall.

Korean War veterans, in the meantime, returned home in silence. The Iron Curtain had been raised. They were quickly forgotten as Korea lingered in a never-resolved ceasefire while a Cold War penetrated our bones, but they too were eventually remembered in 1995 with the Korean War Veterans Memorial. Over twenty thousand American troops are stationed in Korea to this day. Just as we have maintained military bases in Europe and Japan, after World War II to this day. Vietnam War veterans, however, returned to a confused American populous. A memorial to its own veterans helped to heal.

Whether on Veterans Day or Memorial Day—

> Once more join together To celebrate and
> Remember all that could have been
> Remember all that could have been
>
> Let us pray As the day goes down
> White gloves polish And flowers in the park
> March the main streets And the boulevards
> On a Veterans Day
> On a Veteran's Day

Early in 2017 I received a letter from a dear friend, Elliot Goldman:

> *I'm writing you to advise you of a pleasant discussion I had last night with my oldest daughter at dinner. She, and her younger sister and my two grandchildren (14 and 12), have just returned home from a visit to Washington, D.C. While they all were excited about the sights they saw in D.C., she could not stop talking about what was the highlight of their sightseeing which was the Korean War Memorial. While she admired all the memorable sights, it was the enveloping feeling of humanity of the Korean War Memorial that stayed with her, her sister and her children that made the lasting impression.*

In 1991, I had designed the mural with the hopes of engaging all who visited, from a five-year-old to a ninety-five-year-old, to be touched by the service of many, represented by portraits on a wall. The nature of all walls is that people come to them and touch them. People are going to touch the faces of brothers, sisters, and neighbors, in spirit. Kent Cooper said, when he finally saw the mural, "they are so young." I don't know exactly whether it will be in sorrow, in contemplation or in wonder or even joy, but people will be moved. Touch the faces and something from the past will reach your heart. The mural has so many different levels and so many different ways of communicating depending on how you see— with your eyes, hands or with your heart.

President Clinton, Major General Ivany, the Mural and a Soldier

Let us pray as the day goes down
White gloves, polish, and flowers in the park

TEN
DEDICATION

Ceasefire in Korea was proclaimed on July 27, 1953. The Dedication of the Memorial was scheduled for July 27, 1995, forty-two years later. It was a Thursday and one of the hottest and most humid days I've ever experienced. Far greater than the 93°F and 57% recorded for the day. On that bright sunny morning, prior to my radio interview with Harry Smith on CBS News, I walked with Judy down the Mall, parallel to the Reflecting Pool to the memorial. Approaching the Korean memorial, I could see the reflection of the Lincoln Memorial in the mural I created. This was the first time I had seen my work completed, in location, and ready to be viewed by all. It was done and it is beautiful. My eyes welled in tears.

In Korea, since the ceasefire in 1953, there has been continued suffering on all sides. Families who were separated during the "hot war" have seldom been reunited for more than a few days when the actual hostilities stopped. The north and the south were physically devastated as well as emotionally. Most structures were bombed out and unusable. As the months and years passed, each side grew in their separate ways—the North along the militaristic lines of Soviet Russia with the total focus on their leader, Kim Il-sung, and the structure of the state, coupled with vast military marches showing their latest guns and missiles, at other times producing the Arirang Mass Games of synchronized gymnastics. The South withstood the authoritarian repression of Syngman Rhee until he resigned in April 1960 after a series of student and citizen demonstrations resulting in the government proclaiming martial law, suppressing the protests with live fire, eventually opening parliamentary elections and producing a revised constitution which lasted only a year. Today, a satellite photograph at night of the Korean peninsula shows the success of the South's growth after the Korean War—a brightly lighted zone of towns and cities south of the 38th parallel in contrast to the deep dark black area of the north. Business, industry and education thrive in the south.

In 2008 I visited South Korea with Judy, who was performing at the Olympic Stadium. She gave many interviews. I gave a talk at Hongik University; spoke to a graduate class in design—an extraordinary gathering of young creative students striving to be the country's future top designers. Speaking in English (I was asked to wait for a translation, then continue.) After the second or third sequence of this, I didn't wait for the translation . . . and told a joke. The students burst out laughing. They were all well aware and clearly understood English with all its implications. The South Korean economy was brilliant and very much of today. I was told there were 147 undergraduate design programs in South Korea, and more graduate programs from which, together, hundreds of students graduate each year. They all find design jobs, becoming fully employed. Judy and I visited the DMZ, looked across to North Korea, traversing a barren plain of open ground with areas of sparsely growing vegetation. A desolate view of an isolated country, one of terror as it strives for international recognition and nuclear capability. Here is a renewed war threat, not to be forgotten.

Still, the high tension between the North and the South has never ended, with a continuing series of menace from the North over the decades.

Over a million American troops fought in the three year war; 33,739 were killed in combat, 103,284 were wounded. 7,800 are missing-in-action. Killed and missing in the South Korea forces are 217,000 military and over 1,000,000 civilians. North Korea, as best can be estimated lost 406,000 military and 600,000 civilians; and very rough estimates for Communist China are 600,000 military killed. In all, over 2,800,000 million people died, all in three years of war, nearly one million human beings a year. Over the past six decades more than three million Americans have served in Korea. (An accurate number is practically impossible to find through various government sources.) To this day, the United States maintains 28,500 active duty troops in South Korea.

DEDICATION

Looking a few years back, before the dedication, at a groundbreaking on June 14, 1992, another sweltering day, this one a Sunday in Washington, DC. Judy and I met up with Bill Lecky and his wife, Paula, to witness the first President Bush (George H.W. Bush) shovel a spade of dirt, officially breaking the ground for the Korean War Veterans Memorial. All the top military officers and members of Congress were there. Pomp and circumstance. Red, white and blue bunting. It was a special day, but hot in the sun without any shade. Frank Gaylord and Kent Cooper were lost in the crowded stands on the east side. Judy and I sat in the west bleachers with Bill and Paula. The design had been completed, now in final detail development. It was a splendid day for celebration. The program was printed with graphics of the portraits from my mural design. The Foundation Board and the architects, Cooper-Lecky, were mentioned, but not the artists. The program had been printed without noting Frank's or my name.

Eventually, Bob Hansen and the Board assured me that it would be different at the memorial's dedication.

Sometime in 1965, when I was working at Corning Glass designing exhibits, I attended a dinner with a few other designers. My boss's wife, Susan Chiodo, asked us what we were *really* interested in doing. An open question but one that for me was very clear. Others spoke of designing a new product; I spoke of wanting to help people with my designs in whatever their tasks were—working, playing, traveling, living. Today, designing this mural, working with my team in New York, with those in Washington and working with Frank Gaylord in Barre, Vermont was a momentous experience. It seemed evident from the very beginning, before I read Congress's direction that the memorial needed to be all-inclusive. I needed to focus on the people, and today.

On a freezing snow-covered field in Cold Spring, Minnesota in November 1994, I looked for the first time at the full real mural, now completed and set up for final review. Before me, as I had first imagined, and seen in scale mock-ups, was the wall, the mural—over 2,000 photographic portraits of America's men and women serving in the Army, Navy, Marines, Air Force and Coast Guard in Korea between 1950 and 1953, etched onto 41 panels of Academy

Black dark gray highly polished granite, 164 feet long, 12 feet high at one end and 9 inches thick. I could see how it reflected the changing light, how that light behaved differently on the mural throughout the day as clouds moved across the sky. How the blue of the sky and the white clouds and the brilliant snow and the grey of the granite all intermix and changed and changed again, ever moving. All the sampling and set ups in my office and on the streets of Greenwich Village during the previous two and a half years; all the meetings in Barre and Washington, DC, all the trips to Coldspring to verify and work out the grit blasting and the depth of cut, each and every question and adjustment and thought . . . were worth it. In certain lighting conditions and at certain angles, the portraits appeared as negatives, and then quickly change to positives. In a few months, in Washington, at the night after the dedication in 1995, when darkness fell, I would witness the portraits appearing to emerge from within the dark invisible granite, as if the ghosts of those same young men and women were looking out from the past as the granite disappeared. The special lighting helped achieve this, however our custom mezzotint "dot" that integrated the portrait within granular structure of the granite was the prime agent.

All the people at Coldspring granite did a magnificent job—the stonecutters, the grit blast team, the managers and logistics team. Thank you! The juxtaposition of the faces with the snow-covered landscape reflected in the granite was more poignant than I had ever planned or designed. A fitting tribute to the "forgotten war." With admiration and a smile in my eyes, I was filled with pride. From the tens of thousands of faces and figures, here were the ones I had selected, placed, adjusted and lived with, in my New York studio for nearly four years, now standing together, shoulder-to-shoulder on this wind-blown Minnesota plain. The next time I knew I would be seeing them would be in a few months in the heat of July on the National Mall in their "forever" location.

In this time of the Mural and the soldier's figures coming together, I often thought of the different groups of men and women who had been involved in the design of the other memorials on the Mall—of the coffee, cups of tea, the cigarette smoke, morning meetings, the changing seasons, years going by in people's lives as they had in mine—the agreements and the disagreements, children born and parents dying, through changing seasons in the lives of these designers and artists, the intertwining of their daily lives and loves and joys with the construction of memorials that would last far beyond their own lives. In the midst of this work on the Memorial I had lost my stepson, began to plan my wedding, seen some of those whom I loved and cared for pass on—even some of the people who worked with me at the beginning of this memorial process. We all, we artists and designers, engaged in an effort that would bring the sorrows of personal loss to a world of healing. I felt it strongly, and as well I felt the gratitude for being a small part of a great effort, one that would in some way help people in times to come here and heal.

The mural was carefully disassembled by the talented team at Coldspring granite, judiciously wrapped in protective covering, placed on flat beds, and in a convoy of eighteen wheelers, with an escort of Korean War Veterans, made its way to Washington, DC, saluted by veterans and cheered by citizens as it passed through cities and towns along the route from Cold Spring, Minnesota, to the National Mall in Washington, DC.

Sub-contractors, supervised by the Corps of Engineers, began to work on the installation. Curiously, an engineer from the Corps told me and my team that our services were not needed in this phase, that the Corps would review the progress. I understand Cooper-Lecky had been told that they were not needed either. Nor Frank. A couple years later, I found out that lights on the mural would go out, the bushes that were planted were not prospering, and trees were dying for lack of water, all items that our team would have caught were we to supervise. These and other failures, were all gratefully corrected.

The dedication of the memorial was conducted on July 27, 1995, a Thursday and again, one of the hottest and most humid days experienced by many who came to witness. On that bright sunny morning, I walked with Judy down the Mall, parallel to the Reflecting Pool to the memorial. Approaching the Korean War Veterans Memorial, I could see the mural I had created. My heart was in my throat.

As I walked the site of the new Mural, a veteran rushed up to me. I assumed he had seen me being interviewed by CBS News and knew my part in what he was seeing. He grabbed my arm and told me how visiting this new memorial had changed his life forever; forty-two years after his discharge from the Army and his time in Korea, he was now freed from the constraints of the past and discovered a new ability to talk with others about those events long ago, and to see, for himself, what had happened and a different future. Gone was his youth, his innocence, a slice of his life, a shift in his ideals, a time lost in returning to "normal" life. It took the intervening time, between his moment in Korea and that Thursday morning to let himself understand what he had lost, what they had lost, the price they had paid, and he had paid. Finally, he could grieve.

Lives change at a memorial. Ideas change at a memorial. I could already see it happening. "My" mural at the Korean War Veterans Memorial was transforming into "their" mural, "their" memorial—the Korean War Veterans and the American People. Throughout the morning, I listened to more veterans telling their stories. As they stood in front of the mural, they told me that they could feel the cold of the Korean winter and smell the gunfire.

Later that morning, Judy and I walked to the stage set up on a lawn near the Reflecting Pool for her rehearsal with full symphony orchestra and the debut of *Walls*—an anthem she had written using, in part, passages from a poem of mine about Korea. Judy rehearsed the song she would sing that evening to an audience of veterans and foreign dignitaries, the President and First Lady and invited guests from around the country and the world, in celebration of the dedication of the new Memorial. After the rehearsal, we went to the White House to witness the official arrival of the President of Korea, with full ruffle and flourish, a 21-gun salute and the Old Guard Fife and Drum Corps in old traditional Continental Army uniform. We then took a short walk to a luncheon with a few close friends at The Hay-Adams Hotel.

With the afternoon dedication ceremony about to begin, Judy and I found our way to our seats, just to the left rear of the stage, in front of the Mural, amidst soldiers of many nations, the brightest in brilliant yellow dress from Korea. I couldn't see Bill Lecky or Kent Cooper. We were supposed to connect with Frank, but I didn't see him either—all the faces were now merging in the sweltering crowd.

In my mind I could see Henry Bacon and Daniel Chester French at the Lincoln Memorial dedication, probably seated within a few hundred feet of my present location; their feelings of relief and exhilaration must have been profound after such a lengthy process and dealing with all the strong personalities so intimately involved—the many Presidents, the Speaker of the

House, Uncle Joe Cannon. I too had learned that collaboration meant there would always be difficult characters, but they would eventually come around in the face of true splendor.

President Clinton addressed the audience and dedicated the Memorial. I looked around at the maze of people and read through the program. *Again*, my name and Frank Gaylord's were absent from the program. Like many of the other artists and designers through the centuries. At least we were in good company!

The night of the dedication, Judy and I attended a White House dinner in honor of the new memorial and the state visit of the President of Korea, Kim Young-sam. In the receiving line, President Clinton hugged Judy, turned to me with a big smile and put his arm around my shoulder, introduced me to President Kim, told him I had designed the memorial's mural. President Kim bowed to me with clasped hands. I returned his greeting. It was a night of gowns and black ties and uniforms, gold braid and strolling violins. My veteran colleagues were there. And General Ray Davis, the Medal of Honor recipient, then the Lieutenant Colonel who saved a Marine company at the Chosin Reservoir, now president of the Advisory Board and the new Korean War Veterans Memorial Foundation, was seated at President Clinton's table. When I approached Ray to say hello, Katie Couric turned and said, "I know you." And smiled that smile! I smiled a hello, nodded to the President and First Lady. I was seated at another table next to Couric's husband, Jay Monahan.

Judy was seated at the next table over. We had to leave early, breaking with tradition at the White House, to attend the world premiere of Judy singing her new anthem, *Walls*. An usher escorted us to a waiting car and said it was pouring, a drenching rain. Looking at the downpour, we knew the concert would probably be cancelled, but we went to the bandstand anyway. The rain had just stopped. Everyone had dispersed in a great hurry to find shelter from the vicious lightning and thunder and the torrents of water on this extraordinarily hot, humid night, symphony scores and sheet music scattered to the wind. We didn't see a soul. It was strange, but somehow seemed to underscore the entire story of Korea—at once remembered but also forgotten.

Judy wanted to know what I'd like to do the following morning. The Capitol? Perhaps the Holocaust Museum? She had arranged so much for these days, from a luncheon with friends to the brief rehearsal with the symphony orchestra. She suggested we visit the White House. We met up with President Clinton who asked me why "they" wanted to keep the artists a secret. Over the previous five or six years, because of Judy's career and the president's affinity for music, we had become friends; Judy sang at his inauguration concert and one of the Balls. He knew me and wished to mention both my name and Frank Gaylord's in his address but had no idea who the sculptor was and our names were not shown in his briefing papers. The president apologized to me.

That night after the dinner and the dedication, Judy and I were at the memorial, standing with a crowd of people in front of the mural. For the first time I saw the portraits in a faint glow as if floating as ghosts from the past apart from the dark mural wall that had now merged into the darkness of the night. "Listen!" Judy whispered. There was a hushed presence as hundreds of visitors walked and stood at the wall, looking as the ghosts of the past emerge from the invisible granite. A young kid, a teenager, walked past us. "Way cool," he said, "Way cool!" Moments later, I heard the tap of a cane and a muttering as an aged veteran limped past, "They got it right ... they got it right!"

OPPOSITE: The Mural at the Korean War Veterans Memorial, East Section

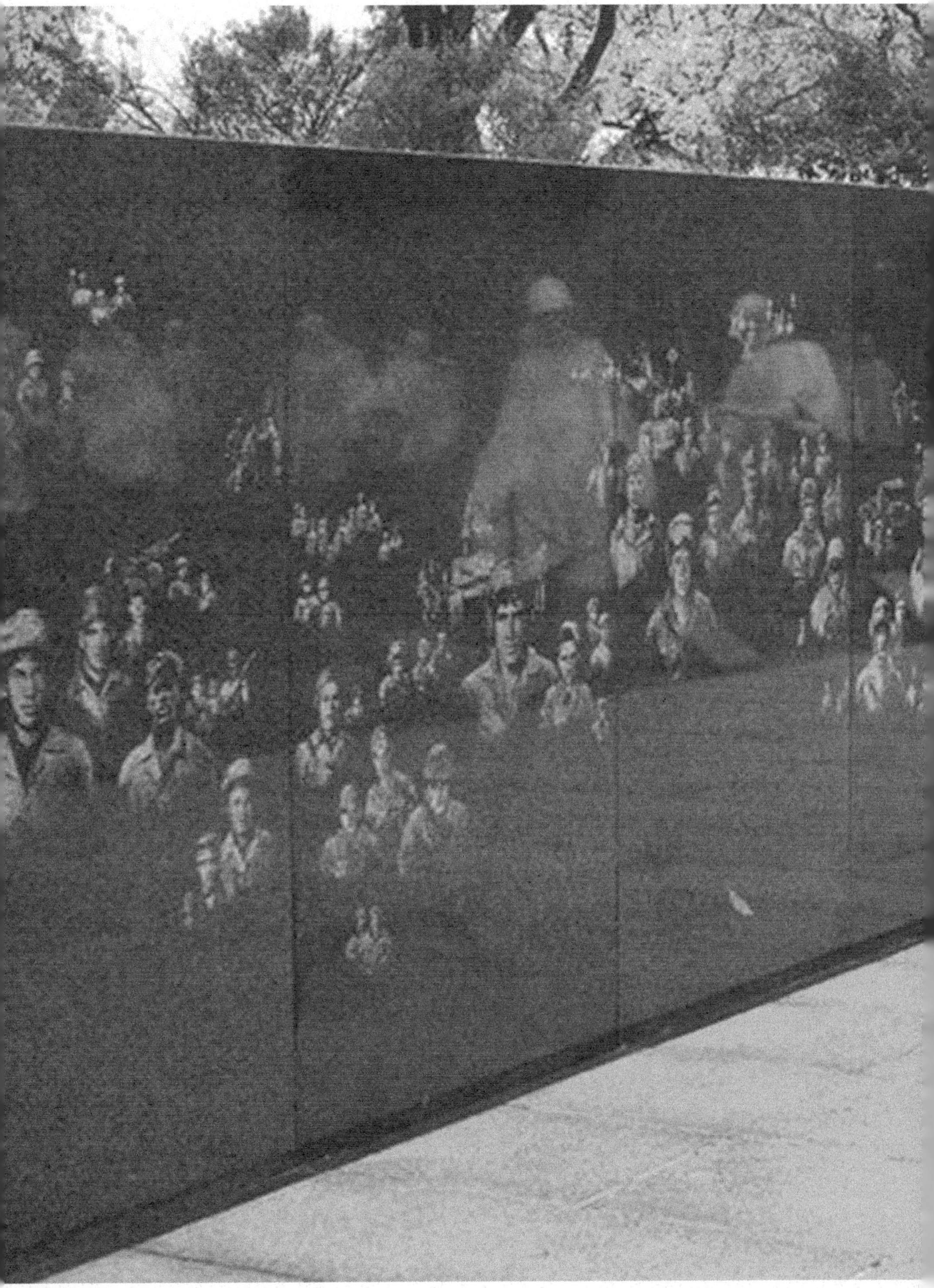

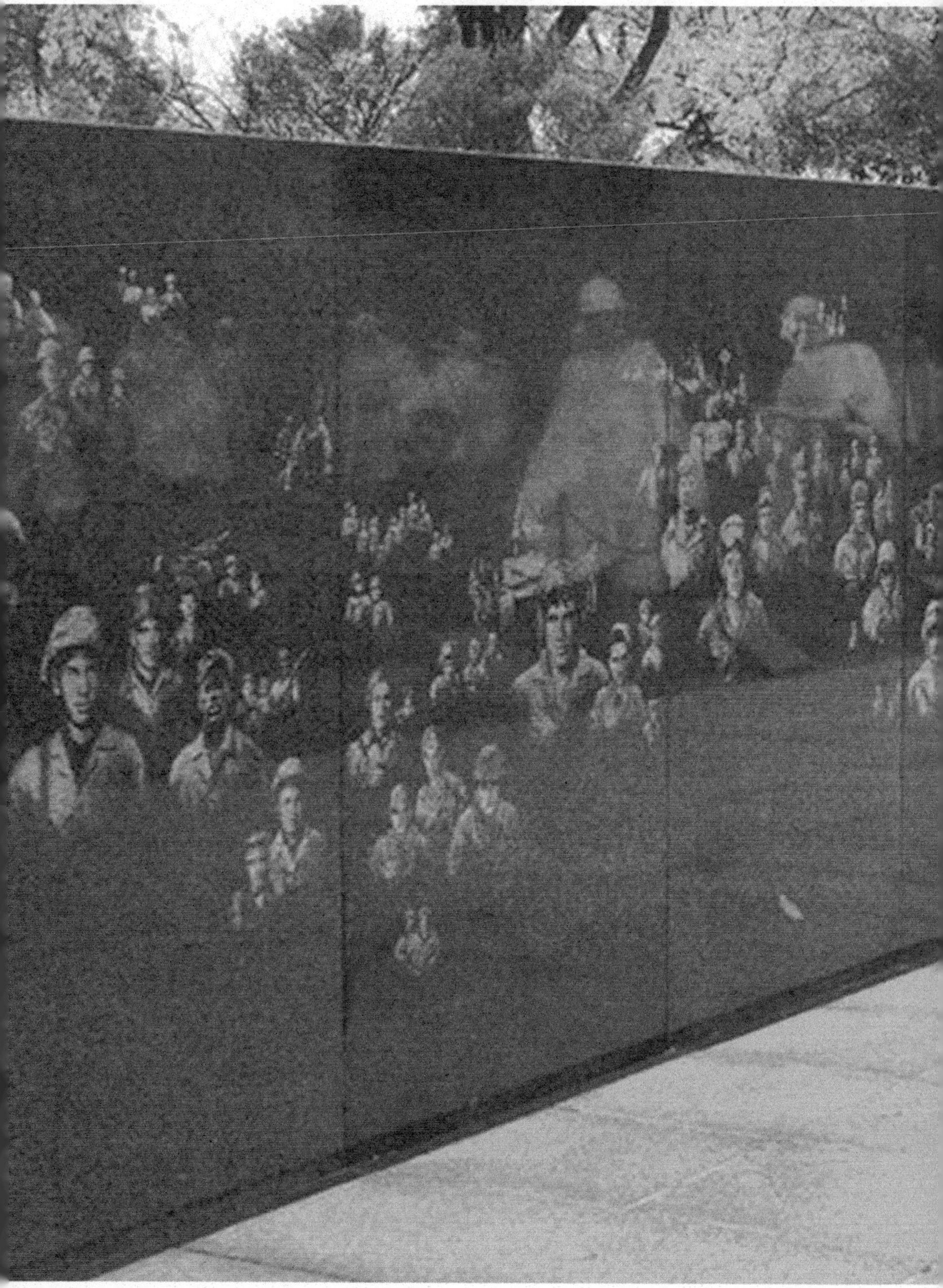

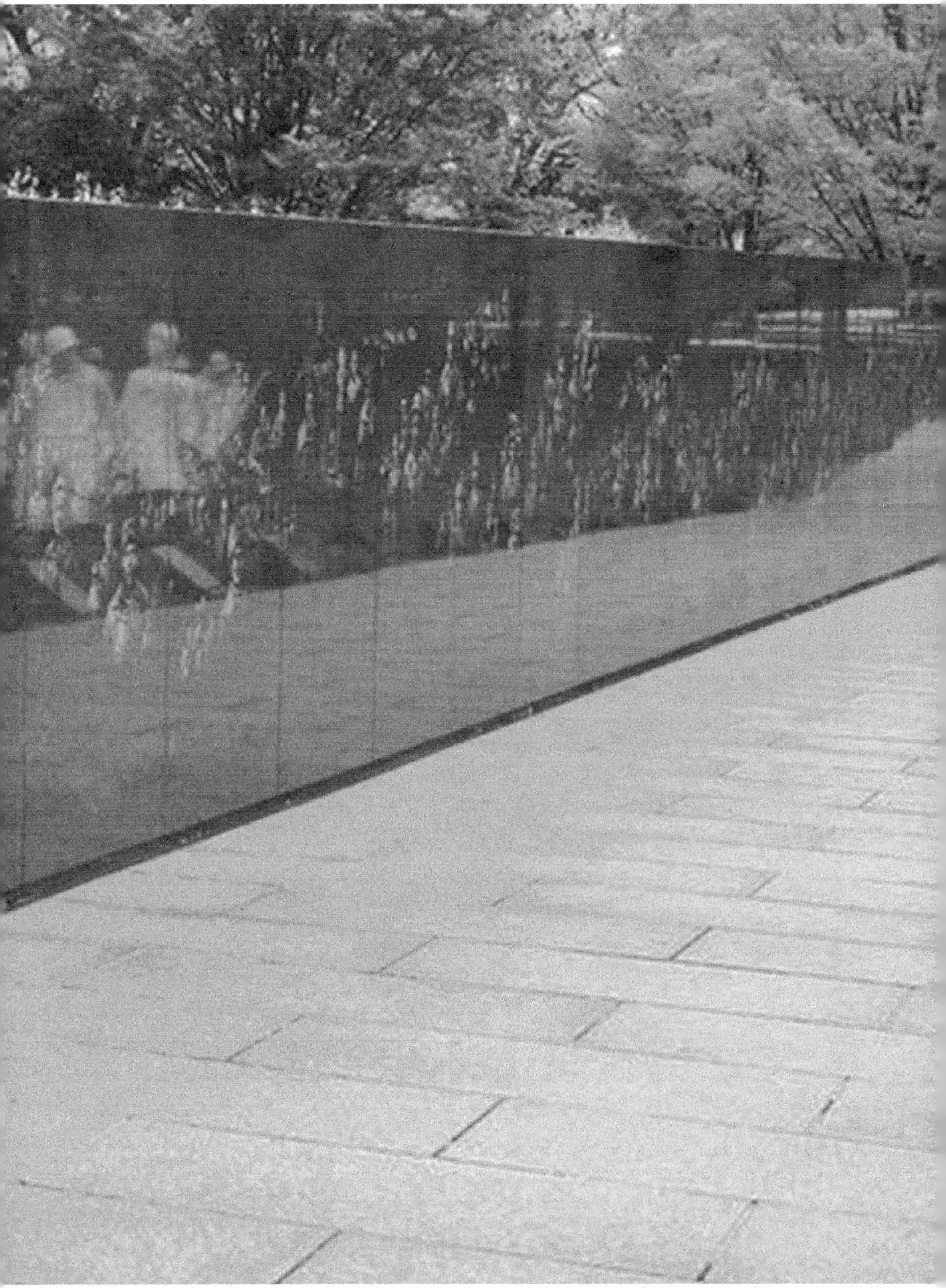

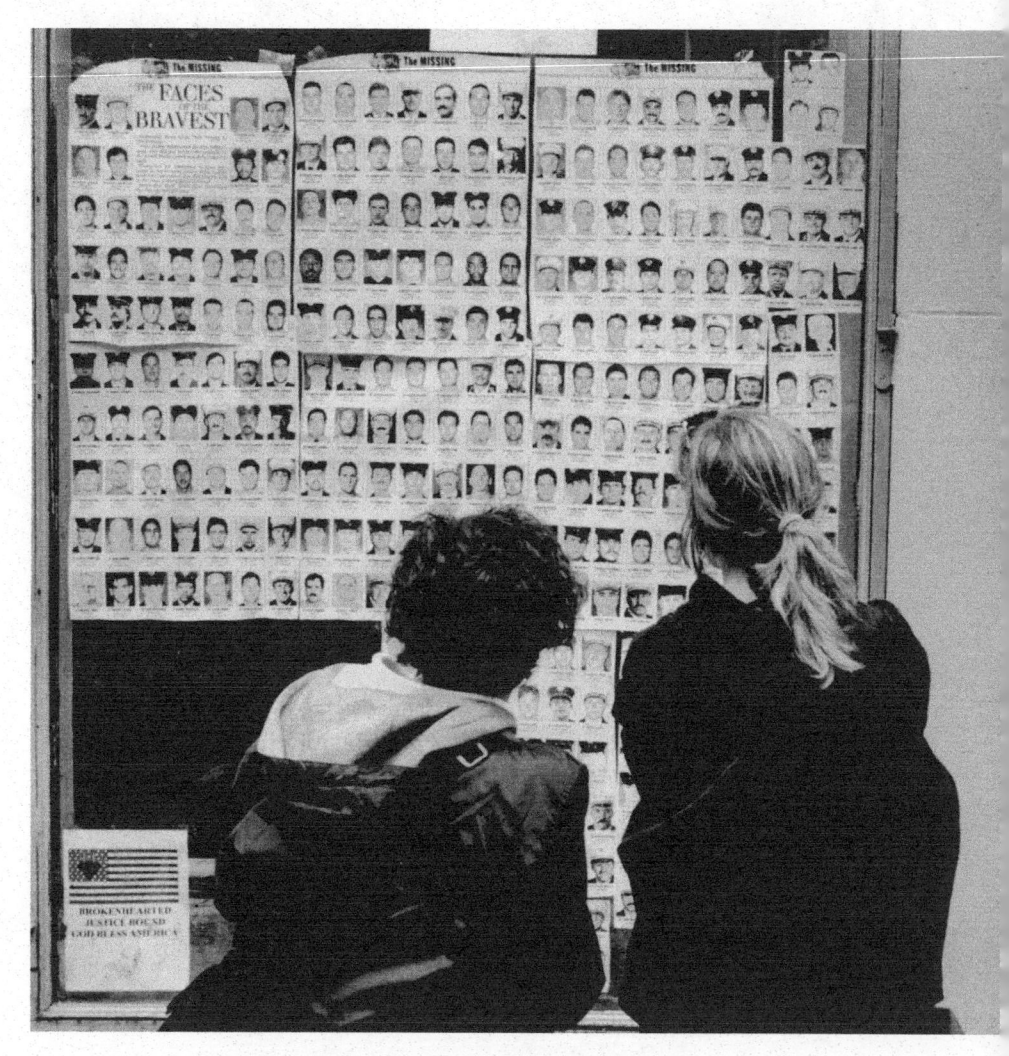

Faces of some of the Missing 9/11 New York

March the main streets and the boulevards
On a Veterans Day
On a Veteran's Day

CODA
MOSAIC

Each morning, when Judy is performing somewhere away from home, here in the States or Europe, perhaps in Australia, I'll write an e-note telling her what I see looking west out my window. I've been doing this for years. One day this past winter, I opened the blinds at 6:15 AM to the calm of a waking day, still dark beyond the Hudson River, lights in a few apartment windows, the streets lamps still a-glow. Looking slightly north, in a blink, like magic, red-magenta sparkles in the window panes, reflecting the rising sun against a midnight blue of the sleeping west. I tell Judy the temperatures here in New York and where she is, in some city in this or another country. In warmer months, the morning sun is bright, just kissing the tops of the buildings across the Hudson River on the Jersey shore. Blue sky and a touch of high cirrus; I feed the kitties Wild Salmon Primavera this morning and tell Judy what will be filling my day; edit another chapter, a meeting to kick off the new K project, form studies for the JB project, water colors if I can get there. The following day, it's a hazy bright morning, the colors mostly soft pastels. Other days after a rain the night before, I see the clean primary colors of morning, the green trees in Riverside Park, a blue ferry going down the Hudson to the World Trade Center, a flash of red somewhere across the Hudson. Surrounding me is my studio. A stack of paper files and books in piles waiting to be read. Sketches pinned on the wall; others taped to the shelves. If I'm at the lake in Connecticut, the outside comes gently inside as Nana said when she first saw it, many years ago. A new freedom through the large window wall. Looking south in the winter, seven deer walk in line across the frozen lake. An hour later they're walking back. New snow falling, looks like I'll drive to the City tomorrow. In summer a heron stands in stillness at the dock, looking down into the water. A Kingfisher rattles from the willow. Chickadees and nuthatches flit at the feeders hanging from branches. Lots of feeders. The sky is blue, stars glitter at night, the Dipper overhead through the trees. Orion clear overhead in the winter night.

Observing... constantly looking. So many things I see. I look. I'm touched as the image touches me—the events in a day, in a life; places I've seen, where I've been, what I've experienced... learned.

The streets of New York. Noise. All too loud. Louder each year. Except after 9/11. Silence then. I could smell the smoke from downtown all the way up here. Walking to the subway in the morning, swaying on the 2 or 3 as it runs downtown. I see what faces me—think of shapes in light and color—people and places. Others listen to their ear buds. A lady offers me a seat. I smile shaking my head, I thank her. Just yesterday a young man did the same. The texture of my old neighborhood across the East River. Roller hockey as a kid, jumping on narrow sidewalks, crowded as I stomp on the lines, "breaking the devil's dishes;" the girls playing Hopscotch. My new baseball uniform, bright in the New York Giants cream color. I like their colors. I was a Yankee fan then. I still like them. Older now. In Manhattan, a fancy doctor's office, looking for a coat hook in the exam room. Remembering the birth of brilliant green glistening from an emerald's light for the first time. And anemones! Oh! The glorious colors. And blue-purple irises. Next visit, still no coat hook. Home now. Music. Joy. I play QXR, afar in the living room so I hear it in interludes when I walk through the apartment to the kitchen. Listen for a moment as I hesitate, caught by a passage. I see Judy, my wife, my best friend, my companion for these many years. Her smile. I remember her smile as I looked across the crowded room years ago. Her eyes speaking to me. I see my friends, colleagues, clients. Their smiles. When I was young, we didn't smile that much. Nor speak much, it seems. Perhaps it was because of the war. Others say it's because we're Norwegian. I learned to understand feelings by the expression in my father's eyes, the turn of my mother's lips. I gathered so much that way. Understood that way. Started to see the expected, the unexpected; delight in the unanticipated, an NYU student's green and yellow hair, a streak of purple as the new semester starts. I see a car that looks as it should, my old Jaguar, different from all the others on the road. Walking through the Met Museum I catch myself smiling. Every time I'm here. I'm suddenly aware of this pleasure, seeing art around me and the joy it brings.

Lingering in my memory, again I see The Green Table *at the Joffrey Ballet, so many years ago. Again, and again while writing this book, Death dancing, marching forever forward, carrying a rippling flag as the diplomats in black sit around a table gesturing. I hear "Pure Imagination" sung by Judy at the Temple of Dendur. Listen to her new song, "Dreamers," hear the joy from my friends. The audiences' eruption into a standing ovation. I see what is there. At times I see what came before... at least I think I do. I see what may be possible; believe what will hopefully move people to understand, to remember, and to act. This is what I do. I'm a designer.*

⁂

Now is a time to see where I've been... how I've changed in these twenty-five years since the memorial's dedication. How we've changed. What we've lived through and what we now face. Korea has changed, both the South and the North. The times will change them even more. Raised in the Depression, reading of World War I and living each war from World War II to this War on Terror, eight major international wars—WWII, Korea, Vietnam, The Cold War, The Gulf, Bosnia and Herzegovina, Afghanistan, Iraq, 9/11, Terror—and numerous smaller yet important conflicts, from Palestine & Israel, Ireland, Kosovo, Rwanda, Syria, and on and on. Social unrest and dissatisfaction; desires by one for a neighbor's possessions, or protecting one's own assets, building strengths, alliances, disagreements, insults, walls, death, weariness, urges for peace, talks, disarmament... the story is so well known. What tools do we have?

The National Security Toolbox... composed of two sections with dividers and folders. First; fortifying borders, strengthening armies, winning an arms race, and having the "ultimate" weapon—the nuclear bomb. And second, on the other side; disarmament, "no-first-strike" agreement, ending arms proliferation, safeguards against accidents, test bans, no underground silos, and of course, the presence of Peacekeepers. What happened to fresh air and adequate water? Joy and Love? Truth and Trust?

⁂

The threat of Korea's 1950 invasion has now, seventy years later, deepened. It's still here, only more intimidating. Is this what happens when peace is not agreed on? When it's kept in abeyance? When people shrug and walk away before the final moment? Could it signal that there will be more episodes to come. The Korean War of 1950 has shifted from our "Forgotten War" to this era's "Seminal War", hastened by Kim Jong-un's continuing quest for the nuclear grail and America's president curious form of combative diplomacy, giving fellow autocrats patience while abandoning and insulting our close friends. A few years ago, South Koreans told me this was an ongoing threat, expressing it in a "matter of fact" manner. Many just shrugged it off. Not now! In 2017, it grew to more concern, with the North's launching missiles and heightened rhetoric, answered in turn by the U.S. president's own bombast. Many of my friends in the United States are growing more concerned with this hostile talk back and forth across the 38th Parallel, where the stability of both leaders is in question. South Korea and Japan remain easy targets. Alaska and Guam have also been threatened, yet we don't hear about them now. Love letters these days. Meanwhile, the North's capabilities continue apace, with the continuing prospect of placing a nuclear device on an intercontinental missile as smaller tactical low-yield nuclear bombs become available. After the first meeting between the American President and Kim Jong-un, the tension had subsided. The second meeting didn't go so well. America, with its allies South Korea and Japan, stopped demonstrations of air and sea power. The U.S. and South Korea resumed joint military exercises in the summer of 2019. So far, there's no real change in the status quo. Not a comforting dialogue to me. Yet, here are the two nations who in 1950, within a few months of engaging in a war, knowingly sought to stop it. Their leaders knew then, perhaps feared, the eventual outcome. Today, with increased tension, and uncertainty between both countries, the Korean War Veterans Memorial enters a renewed focus for some individuals and moves to be an uneasy reminder of an earlier time.

As I look around me, I see the basic standard of what we each hold sacred, the firm ground we can depend on... shifting. A promise of security after 9/11 has now shifted once again into greater uncertainty. What lessons can we learn as we view the war memorials on the Mall, from Korea to Vietnam? From Washington to Lincoln? From our Wars and from their Leaders? From all the people who have visited these memorials and monuments these past decades!

I trust in what I have designed, I see how my designs have helped the people of America—in food choices, transportation ease, entertainment, information and finding one's way. Somehow, our team had brought into being a new form of memorial that is far from a "man-on-a-horse" or a statue on a pedestal or a portrait on a mantelpiece. I see Korea and the other monuments designed and built by dedicated individuals brought together for a common purpose: Robert Mills, Daniel Chester French, Henry Bacon, Maya Lin, Kent Cooper and Bill Lecky, Frank Gaylord, and me, Louis Nelson, and our teams. In our time, each of us have stood for what we've believed in, for a struggle that in the end was worth every effort—whether forgotten or remembered, and for the promise of peace after a war.

Still, I'm not satisfied.

I see more hate amongst us. More intolerance of the differences between us, not the similarities. More impatience. Pushing in a crowd, a rush, beeping of horns. Hate and fear of the difference of color, nationality, wealth and creed. Others express this as an embarrassment of populist nativism; xenophobic anti-Semitic authoritarianism. Hate and extremism. We see it in the news, in the gathering of groups and their opposition, in name calling and bullying, even from the highest office; in the action of authorities such as our police. Expressions of ethnic nationalism in a need to explain failures, rally masses and up-end meritocracy. Some must shoot and kill unsuspecting individuals, children in schools, houses of worship and places of learning and entertainment, all shared grounds. Yet, a woman offers her seat to a man on the subway, each a different color. Can things be all that bad?

I live with a promise of peace after war each morning, ready to work on what I can do and achieve today, with each step that will enhance my life—and our lives—for the better. Just one step to help make a change that matters. That's the promise I see in each sunrise as I prepare for the events of the day, taking care of the order of things—from making my bed and brushing my teeth to feeding my cats; from writing the ending for this book to initiating the next mindful ideas for the evolving projects in front of me; from painting a watercolor or making a wire sketch to getting on the treadmill to limber my muscles and increase my heart rate, do floor stretches, taking care of myself so that I may take my next step.

It was vital to review the paths of war and reflect on earlier means to resolve differences and avoid wars. I trust the reader will come to understand the dramatic change in America's history of war. Korea started a period of military setbacks and challenges, stalled in a ceasefire that continues to this day. The process through the Vietnam War, the Gulf War in Iraq, Afghanistan and the long Second Persian Gulf War; shifting to a War on Terror with Al-Qaida and now, ISIS, leads to a serious global threat as Putin and Russia annexes the Crimea from Ukraine while their jets fly dangerously close to NATO forces and western support in Syria, a country now devastated with internal strife. All while we at home are seemingly paralyzed in a stalemate more costly than the standoff in Korea. Do the leaders want peace or must they need an extra pound of flesh?

Can we distill an essence of peace from this string of wars and understand why Korea and the Korean War of so long ago and its Veterans Memorial shout a silent alarm?

Underlying our daily routines, my family and I and so many of us, perhaps all of us, are living with a constant sense of uncertainty for the first time in many years; a persistent fear of war that we once knew after World War II and during the long Cold War; and a terror in our midst since September 11th, 2000. And what what will happen next in Washington? Those earlier feelings, as I imagine, must have led Wilson to the creation of The League of Nations, and subsequently, Roosevelt to initiate the United Nations and Truman and others to bring forth NATO, all international organizations intended to limit that fear, if not bring to this world, peace . . . and of course, a peace within our own government. It's dismaying to again take on this cloak of uncertainty and not have the trust in our leader to restore a sense of hope for peace.

Historically, only a few American presidents have pulled us out of war or nearly done so, one losing his life in the process. Roosevelt, near-death, helped to negotiate peace at Yalta, Truman tried to right a wrong in Korea, and Eisenhower pressed for a truce in the war, stopping the killing while allowing for an unsettled difference between two peoples of the same culture that reverberates more loudly today. Kennedy staying calm, maintained a "stand-by" while he and Khrushchev contained the Cuban Missile Crisis. As for his intentions for Vietnam, they became still-born with his assassination; Kennedy had intended to reduce the number of troops in Vietnam by the end of 1963, as well as carry on a secret dialogue with Khrushchev—the purpose of which was purportedly to lessen the tension between the two nations. Johnson enacted most of Kennedy's social agenda, brought to us all, the Great Society and social reform and freedoms to America, while concurrently intensifying the disaster in Vietnam and expanding America's commitment, feeding our youth to that effort. Nixon advanced that strategy, eventually got us out of Vietnam as he got out of the White House by the skin of his teeth. Reagan went to Reykjavik, Iceland to meet with Gorbachev, together opening an international door eventually leading to limiting nuclear weapons . . . and the world could start to breathe again. Time marched on, Clinton sent Richard Holbrooke to mediate peace in Bosnia and Herzegovina, resulting in the Dayton Accords and did the same in asking George Mitchell to look at ending The Troubles in Northern Ireland; Clinton wished he had done more for Rwanda. And Obama sought to extract us from Iraq with the daily loss of lives, tiring our citizens for questionable results, eventually setting the steps to remove us from Afghanistan—never taking those steps to right two misconceived wars based on unconfirmed intelligence and misguided strategies from the previous administration, costing thousands of American youth, leaving America exposed and hated by many, only now to look back into Afghanistan while Iraq continues to garner our attention alongside a demolished Syria, as Damascus stands, untouched. And our current president betrays our allies and turns traitor to those who fought for the United States in Syria while he casts more lies to enhance his personal benefit over the needs of our country. Who knows what the next steps of ISIS will be, or if ISIS will merge into something else with car bombs and suicide bombers and trucks on a rampage? Who knows what the next memorial will be to satisfy our people? A War on Terror Memorial is being discussed at this moment.

Even with this shorthand history, the link between then and now excites us each day; the curious connection between living at the edge in fear and witnessing the uncertainties from afar, at a safe distance.

In the months following the Korean War Veterans Memorial dedication in 1995, I received letters and notes, and many emails. I was pleased to receive a letter from Hillary Rodman Clinton saying that she and Chelsea had gone one night incognito to visit the memorial, felt very moved and wanted to send me their congratulations again. Another letter arrived from Madeleine Albright, then Secretary of State, who told me how much she admired my design; she also related the comments of the other visitors who had been there with her, a twelve-year-old, "a future leader" as the Secretary called her, was inspired to tell her grandparents about her experience, standing amidst the people of the Korean War Veterans Memorials and how the memory of it will live with her.

Over these years I've also received letters from family members of the Korean veterans; I heard from a granddaughter who thanked me for my design and asked if her grandfather was one of the faces in the mural. A number of days ago, an email from Colonel Todd Wood, now working at the Pentagon, asking if his grandmother's brother, Junior D. Edwards, a Medal-of-Honor recipient was on the wall, a resemblance to a photo he holds. All these messages tell me that many have visited the memorial and wanted to learn more, and that they were honored to have had a relative who had served for their country, and for them.

These are monuments to our loss, but also to the triumph of the human heart. Blood and beauty rest on this Mall—hope and challenge—the moments that mark a history. The psychiatrist and diagnostician M. Scott Peck writes, "Our extraordinary capacity for *transformation* is the most essential characteristic of human nature. It is both the basic cause of war and the basic cure for war."

Living my life exposes me to new thoughts in art and technology . . . as well as to a friend's story . . . and to how we can live to each other's benefit. Living sways what we see, what is logical, what is at the edge and what is acceptable and achievable. It is far more potent than driverless cars; yet driverless cars can bring meaning to our lives. They influence those who plan, those who design and those who have a vision to express and create the places that liberates each of us. We live along a time continuum. As surely as we age, it takes longer to walk across the street by the time the "DONT WALK" or "HAND" flashes in red. The planner knowing this need will adjust the time sequence in changing the red and green lights, which will affect the driving time from one place to another in the city, affecting many other lives and whether we're late or on time in our own sequence of planning. Even as I write this, I know that my feelings are changing, slowly—then instantly, in the blink of an eye. Still, many stand with both feet on the ground in the comfort of our traditions.

It is a worthy tradition to settle all disputes and bring harmony. In one of my recovery programs we make "amends" to settle an issue. Others have a tradition to keep the disagreements and animosity alive through generations to come. I'd vote for peace and understanding. "True reconciliation does not consist in merely forgetting the past," said Nelson Mandela. And not live through the "Troubles" or the ageless fight in Jerusalem. So, why not resolve the ongoing conflict between North and South Korea and move on so that all sides can come to some settlement about the things they need and get on with living? This seems where the two nations are inching toward with hiccups along the way.

Ideally, in a negotiation, both or all parties should walk away as a "winner," each obtaining what they need. That's a long step, probably many steps from the list of demands held by two parties in their national security toolboxes, among the tools of war and the instruments of peace. For some, the nuclear weapon is the only real deterrent—along with fortifying borders, strengthening armies and winning the arms race. What about retaining clean water and safe breathable air? Education our children? What then leads to both sides winning? The astuteness of the negotiator/mediator . . . a new George Mitchell—the man who helped to solve the Irish "Troubles," enabling each party to see the opportunities and avoid a fight, even after decades of animosity and battles across the hedges or in a court.

It is a giant step to understand the meaning of these interconnections, these pieces and how we are positioned in this mosaic. Yet, we've lived through all this before, haven't we . . . at least some of us have. I look back at the patterns that I have written about and the individuals who were pressed into action by their beliefs—John Newton, William Wilberforce, George Washington, Alexander Hamilton, Thomas Jefferson, Benjamin Franklin, James Madison, John Quincy Adams, Abraham Lincoln, Daniel Webster, Winston Churchill, Franklin Roosevelt, Harry Truman, Dwight D. Eisenhower, John F. Kennedy, Martin Luther King Jr., Robert Kennedy, Lyndon B. Johnson, Ronald Reagan, Bill Clinton, Barack Obama and the thousands of Junior D. Edwards with them. Individual rights. Human rights. Freedom and liberty. Through the periods in which they lived—the Revolutionary War, Civil War, World War I and World War II, the Korean War, the Cold War, the Cuban Missile Blockade, the Vietnam War, the Gulf War, the wars in Iraq and Afghanistan—leading you and me, dear reader, to this day. Today. Each of these individuals sought to do what was right and tied themselves to a thread, fixed themselves into the grout of the mosaic.

Frank Gaylord sculpted nineteen warriors for the Korean War memorial; I found over two thousand portraits of men and women in our Armed Services and placed them in a 140 foot long mural; General Richard Stilwell fought to his death to get this built; and Colonel Rosemary McCarthy assured that women would be remembered in this memorial. Lieutenant Colonel Ray Davis led his men through a freezing hell and saved many more, telling me they were "resolute." Pete Seeger sang of freedom, of Paul Robeson's song being silenced in 1949 by the Klu Klux Klan in Peekskill, New York, the year before the Korean War started while the police flaccidly looked on. Yet, with the Klan active in the South, and while diligently pursuing the South's "Lost Cause," Georgia's Richard Russell Jr. chairing the Senate's investigation into the firing of General Douglas MacArthur, asked penetrating questions of MacArthur, who was newly relieved of command of the Korean War. The General's dubious answers quelled the Senate's and the public's attacks on Truman who had fired MacArthur when the General threatened to enlarge the war with a bombing attack on China (perhaps using a nuclear weapon), forever weakening the public's view of MacArthur, the hero five-star general who had hopes to run for President of the United States.

That thread pulls them together, weaves me into a new world tapestry, a mosaic story, perhaps a puzzle we together are building.

Much of the cycle of war and redemption is written into the simple story of Cain and Abel. Yet as I see it, Cain and God had worked out a deal. They negotiated a settlement. A negotiation with God ... or that's the way the scribes of old wrote it and others translated the story. And that deal proceeds to this day, enduring the flood. Abel may be forgotten while Cain and the act of murder are remembered, memorialized, as is the mystery of the acceptance of sin in the presence of offerings to God. One might even surmise, in the "inevitability of war," that the power of Cain is commemorated and honored.

Not so! There is redemption for Abel—a memorial for Abel. Abel takes on the mantle of the good for us all. For those who have worked hard to provide a life for their children. There is a memorial for the innocent one who served. The "just" survive as victor in many instances. Yet, the toll mounts. Comrades and loved ones grieve. A remembrance is conducted. A memorial is built.

With the men who brought us war and death, we commemorate *their* war. And *our* loss.

During the Lincoln-Douglas debates in 1858, Lincoln said, "It is the eternal struggle between these two principles—right and wrong—throughout the world.... It is the same spirit that says, 'You toil and work and earn bread, and I'll eat it." No matter in what shape it comes, whether from the mouth of a king who seeks to bestride the people of his own nation, and live by the fruit of their labor, or from one race of men as an apology for enslaving another race, it is the same tyrannical principle."

Monuments and memorials do have the power to change lives. I wish more of our leaders would come to these places and spend a meditative moment. I trust some have come here and experienced those moments in solitude, bringing their own thoughts of conflict and unease to Lincoln, Vietnam and Korea. Perhaps in them they see some form of hope. What happens then as they go back to the White House or the Senate or the House of Representatives... and reengage in the tussles of ego and entrenchments? How can that change?

Time can suffocate a silent public. History has charted the timelines as many are killed. We write songs, make plays, dance dances. And build memorials. The story is not about the memorial, but about the people of the memorial. Not about the stone and bronze, but about the blood. Not about the moment, but about endurance. Not of yesterday, but of tomorrow. Not of what happened, nor why it happened, but how we have changed and grown because of it.

For in struggle is growth, lest we stay in the past seeking revenge and retribution. We seek wisdom, we hope. The process of war and death moves on and on, through centuries, hooked in its own thread.

This is the time to look forward, not over our shoulder. To look through the mirror for the promise of this new era forced upon us. This is the time to cherish and protect this fragile thread of connections linking us to those we know little about. A colored multifaceted mosaic of pieces that seem to fit and tell a story. These new tentative steps will tell us more about ourselves, about each person, each family, each community. Constant in all, looking through the mirror at the interconnected places we see, the man-on-a-horse sits astride his steed, silent, resolute and waiting, never looking back, always looking steadfastly... resolutely to our horizon.

We only gain the future when we remember the past.

Louis Nelson
August 2020

The Reflecting Pool at Twilight

SUPPLEMENT

Veteran's Day. Michael Veitch. Lyrics. 171

Acknowledgements. Thank You 173

Resources. Bibliography 177

Walls Arise. Poem. Louis Nelson 181

WALLS. Words by Judy Collins and Louis Nelson. 183

Remembering the 'Forgotten War'
Washington Post Op-Ed. July 1995 185

Designers of National Memorials &
Monuments on the National Mall (partial list) 187

Glossary of Acronyms and Abbreviations 189

Citation for Medal of Honor. Raymond G. Davis 191

The Author. Louis Nelson 195

VETERAN'S DAY

As performed and recorded by Judy Collins, May 4, 2011

This is to all who find themselves
Not playing on the old school yard
Running for their lives
And not much else
To the drumming of their own desperate hearts
To the drumming of their own desperate hearts

Its blood and bullets now on our minds
The times they never change that much
Come a day we'll honor all those who have died
And remember the less fortunate ones
Remember the less fortunate ones

Let us pray as the day goes down
White gloves, polish, and flowers in the park
March the main streets And the boulevards
On a Veterans Day
On a Veteran's Day

The Sky tries smiling,
Painted up, dry leaves flying
I can't stop wishing a rainbow

Before the last flood washes over us
To leave us here on the sweet ground
Once more join together to celebrate and
Remember all that could have been
Remember all that could have been

Let us pray As the day goes down
White gloves, polish, and flowers in the park
March the main streets And the boulevards
On a Veterans Day
On a Veteran's Day

Michael Veitch
Burt Street Music (BMI)

ACKNOWLEDGEMENTS

THANK YOU

I wrote a poem in 1995. Soon it was edited and added to by Judy Collins, turned into a song that grew into an anthem, eventually orchestrated for a full symphony. In those years, I had been reading Billy Collins as a day-reader, one poem a day. I still do. Earlier, I read Robert Pinsky, Robert Bly and others. I exercised to Joseph Campbell and *The Hero With a Thousand Faces*. 9/11 happened and I was asked to write an article about memorials for New York magazine. With all good intentions, that writing grew into an idea for a book… that never got started until Jerry Mundis broke the log jam and opened the road, kicking me into the writing process. Thank you, each and every one.

From writing proposals for the designs I created, I started to write about memorials. Those pages raised many themes, forming chips building the power of memorials, the futility of war and the promise for redemption—a mosaic of colors and textures.

I'm grateful beyond words for the gifts from my mother and father, Ingrid Godfreida Gjersdal Nelson and Louis Nelson and my sister Dorothy Nelson and her partner, Elaine Vogt. As well, for an early journey with Jeanne Caffrey (Dr. Jeanne N. Ketley) and another with Sandra Balestracci (Sandra Balestracci Boucher). Thank you. And to my teachers, Rowena Reed Kostellow, who taught me of design and life and Max Margulis, of the power of my voice.

Over the years, I've listened to Judy Collins, read her lyrics, savored Robert Caro's volumes on Moses and Johnson, learned from Ron Chernow of the giants and read much of Gay Talese. Then, there is my design staff, particularly Krista Briese and Hai Phung Tran, who were a constant help with photographs and refreshing my memory. Angela DeDominick smoothed the logistics and details as this manuscript grew. I'm thankful for William Clark's encouragement as he searched for a publisher in the beginning; Walt Bode, who early in the process gave my book idea a structure; and Suzanne Oaks, who asked about the "man on a horse." Lorna Owens, my editor today, brought my revised book idea into a manageable form, guiding me into a new book; Mike Di Paola looked at each line and checked each fact, Margery Cantor encased it with a splendid design.

I'm grateful to Loretta Barrett, now gone, for reading my book ideas again and again, giving me notes, meeting with me over many lunches around 23rd Street, pointing a way; Dean James Park (Jim) Morton for talking with me about the search for peace, the fragility and strength of a human life; and Dean James A. (Jim) Kowalski for clarifying the Genesis story, both Jims are shepherds, at different times Dean at the Cathedral Church of Saint John the Divine in New York.

I'm thankful for all who discussed the process of writing with me and those who read my manuscript in its various editions through the years, advising along the way: Judy Collins, Susan Cheever, Mort Sheinman, Harold Holzer, Sheila Weller, John Kelly, Charles Salzburg, Bob Lascaro, Larry Altman, John Glusman, Nina Weiner, Lawrence Schiller, William Norwich, Ron Chernow, Lionel Tiger, Dean Jim Kowalski, Tucker Viemeister, RitaSue Siegel, Dean Clifton Daniel III, Bishop Andrew Dietsche, Erica Jong, Molly Jong Fast, Jonathan F. Fanton, Bill Kelly, Susan Eisenhower, Gay Talese; and Nan Talese who frequently read my manuscripts and offered thoughts and recommendations; for Jonathan Fanton telling me not to delete a personal story; and David Black who surprised me with a draft screen play from his reading my manuscript; Joan Hamburg insisting I find what was served at The Dinner on Maiden Lane; and Jim ... James Hart who mentioned, "take what you want ..."; for Jeremy Hooper who found the missing piece; and for the vision of Katherine DePaul, who talked with me about bringing *Mosaic* to my public.

I'm indebted for my photo collaborators, Toby Old, Elizabeth Freund and an unidentified US Army photographer; to Andy Kropa and Adam Hitt for getting the tone just right; to Scott French and his group who helped me understand their unique process; Matthew Idler, for his assistance in printing and publishing this book and the staff of BookBaby.

To the veterans of the Korean War and the Korean War Veterans Memorial Advisory Board, led by retired Gen. Richard G. Stilwell and Medal of Honor recipient retired Gen. Raymond G. Davis, and Executive Director Robert L. Hanson—all three now gone; Col. William E. Weber, now retired from leading the Board; and the Board members, all retired from the military... Col. Rosemary T. McCarthy, now departed, Col. James McKevitt, also gone who earlier suggested I look at the history of the Lincoln Memorial, John Phillips who told me of his time near Old Baldy in Korea, James Butcher, Lt. Col. Jim Fisher, Lt. Gen. Bernard Champoux and many others on the Advisory Board, all retired from active duty, many who are reflected in these pages.

Nancy Lascheid, in an email and then a conversation told me about her husband, Dr. Bill Lascheid's service in Korea, then provided me with a copy of his memoir. I'm most grateful.

Frank Gaylord, Bill Lecky and Kent Cooper, my co-designers and artists of the Korean War Veterans Memorial, and John Triano on Frank Gaylord's team; Jennifer Stoller, who worked closely with me and my staff; Linda Christenson who found each and every photograph for me (and thousands more) to build this design and tell this story, and to the Coldspring granite team, led by Dan Rea who made the design real.

Maj. Gen. Robert Ivany and the Army War College staff who showed me Gettysburg; Lt. Col. (Ret) Ruth B. Collins at the Army War College Foundation who gave advice and found experts to advise me along the way.

Barbara Weisberg for giving me *Lincoln at Gettysburg;* Bill Moyers, who gave me Richard Whelan's *Drawing the Line* and asked about the Daniel Webster sculpture in Central Park; Michael Veitch for writing *Veteran's Day* and giving me permission to use it my way; my dear friend Robert Caro, who brought clarity to my understanding parts of American history in his *Years of Lyndon Johnson.*

To Dr. Nancy Coles for assuring I will continue to see all that surrounds me; and all my other doctors and specialists who looked, measured, prodded, advised and prescribed for my health and fitness; Stanley S. Schrem, Morton Leibowitz, H. Leon Pachter, Charles J. Lightdale, Blair S. Lewis, Lawrence J. Caprio, Nathan Rabhan, Richard Ash, Lawrence J. Calagna and Riva; Barbara Quinn, Yvette E. Obadia, Florence Knopf and my dear friend, Lawrence K. Altman for his thoughts on many matters; as well as all the others who have helped me near and far.

To all the friends of Bill and Bob who have shared their experience, strength and hope with me over my decades in the program.

And to our three Persian muses, Tom Wolfe, Coco Chanel and Rachmaninoff, for their silent devoted company sitting with me during my many hours and years writing and pondering at the computer screen, looking out the window at the passing helicopters and boats on the Hudson.

But mostly, all in all, to Judy Collins, my life companion, wife and closest friend, for constantly encouraging me, telling me to tell the story, make it more personal, add more details about the people and places, the color, the weather and the smiles, not to preach, and to sit up and take a walk; to move that piece up front, and also this story, and the other one, too; for reading the many versions of the manuscript, asking in the next-to-last read, "who is Jeanne," editing the last edition, offering her thoughts—most taken gladly... and eventually, every single one. I am grateful for our life together. Thank you, Sweetheart!

Love you all,
Louis
2 August 2020

RESOURCES/BIBLIOGRAPHY

Altman, Lawrence K. *Who Goes First?* Random House. 1987.
Berdik, Chris. "Petraeus May Have Been Felled by His Own Brain Chemistry." *The Daily Beast.* November 17, 2012.
Blair, Clay. *The Forgotten War.* Anchor Press Doubleday. 1987.
Brady, James P. *The Coldest War.* Orion Books, New York. 1990.
Brooks, David. Column. *New York Times.* October 16, 2017.
Broyles Jr, William. Why Men Love War. *Esquire,* November 1984.
Campbell, Joseph. *The Hero with a Thousand Faces.* New World Library. 1949. Reprinted 2008.
Caro, Robert A. *The Path to Power. The Years of Lyndon Johnson.* Vintage. 1981.
_____. *Means of Ascent. The Years of Lyndon Johnson.* Vintage. 1990.
_____. *Master of the Senate. The Years of Lyndon Johnson.* Knopf. 2002.
_____. *The Passage of Power. The Years of Lyndon Johnson.* Knopf. 2012.
Carpenter, Teresa, Editor. *New York Diaries. 1609 to 2009.* Modern Library, New York. 2012.
Cerami, Charles A. *Dinner at Mr. Jefferson's.* John Wiley & Sons, Inc. 2008
Chernow, Ron. *Alexander Hamilton.* Penguin, 2004.
_____. *Washington. A Life.* Penguin, 2010.
_____. *Grant.* Penguin, 2017.
Collins, Judy. *The Judy Collins songbook,* Grosset & Dunlap, 1969.
_____. *Voices.* Clarkson Potter, 1992. With CD.
_____. *The Seven T's.* Tarcher/Penguin, 2007.
_____. *Sweet Judy Blue Eyes,* Crown Archetype, 2011.
_____. *Cravings.* Nan A. Talese/Doubleday, 2017.

Collins, Judy and Nelson, Louis. *Walls (We Are Not Forgotten)*. Wildflower. 1995.

Copland, Aaron. *Lincoln Portrait*. 1942.

Davis, Wade. *Into The Silence*. Alfred A. Knopf, 2011.

Donald, David Herbert. *Lincoln*. Simon Schuster, 1995.

Edelman, Bernard. Editor. *Dear America*. W.W. Norton & Co. 1985.

Ellis, Joseph J. *Founding Brothers*. Alfred A Knopf. New York, 2000.

_____. *Revolutionary Summer*. Alfred A. Knopf. New York, 2013.

Ferling, John. *Jefferson and Hamilton*. Bloomsbury Press, 2013.

Fox, Emmet. *Around the Year with Emmet Fox*. Harper Collins. 1992.

Gelb, Leslie. "The Forgotten Cold War: 20 Years Later, Myths about the U.S. Victory Persist." *Daily Beast*, 23 December 2011.

Grum, Bernard. *The Timetables of History*. Simon & Schuster, 1991.

Gugliotta, Guy. "New Estimate Raises Civil War Death Toll." *New York Times*, Tuesday, April 3, 2012.

Halberstam, David. *The Best and the Brightest*, Random House, 1972.

_____. *The Next Century*. Harper Collins, 1992.

_____. *War In A Time Of Peace*. Scribner, 2001.

_____. *The Coldest Winter*. Hyperion, New York, 2007.

Halprin, Lawrence. *The Franklin Delano Roosevelt Memorial*. Chronicle Books, 1997.

Hannah, Gail Greet. *Elements of Design*. Princeton Architectural Press, 2002.

Highsmith, Carol M. & Landphair, Ted. *Forgotten No More*. Chelsea Publishing, 1995.

Hinshaw, Arned L. *Heartbreak Ridge Korea, 1951*. Pocket Books, 1989.

Holzer, Harold, *Lincoln and the Power of the Press*. Simon & Schuster, 2014.

_____. *Monument Man*. Princeton Architectural Press. 2019.

Hochschild, Adam. *To End All Wars*. Houghton Mifflin. 2011.

Holy Bible. *King James Version*. Zondervan. 2001.

Janney, Peter. *Mary's Mosaic*. Skyhorse Publishing, 1012.

Kirsten, Lincoln. Afterword. *W. Eugene Smith, An Aperture Monograph*. 1969. Aperture Foundation. 1969.

Langworth, Richard M., Editor *Churchill's Wit*. Ebury Press. 2009.

Larson, Erik. In *The Garden of Beasts*. Crown, 2011.

Lecky, William P. FAIA. *Designing for Remembrance*. LDS Publishing, 2012.

Lessard, Suzannah. *The Architect of Desire*. Dell. 1996.

_____. *The Absent Hand*. Counterpoint. 2019.

Levine, Stephen. Various Books on Death and Healing.

MacMillan, Margaret. *Paris 1919*. Random House, 2001.

Maddow, Rachel. *Drift*. Crown, 2012.

Mandel, Susan. "The Lincoln Conspirator." *The Washington Post*, February 3, 2008.

Maraniss, David. *They Marched Into Sunlight*. Simon & Schuster, 2003.

National Park Service. *Memorial Web Sites*. 2008.

Newton, Jim. *Eisenhower: The White House Years*. Anchor Books. 2012.

Peck, M. Scott. *Meditations from the Road*. Touchstone. Simon & Schuster, 1993.

Reston, Jr. James. *Warriors of God: Richard the Lionheart and Saladin in the Third Crusade*. Anchor. 2001.

_____. *A Rift in the Earth*. Arcade Publishing. 2017.

Richman, Michael. *Daniel Chester French*. The Preservation Press, 1976.

Sears, Stephen W. *Gettysburg*. Houghton Mifflin Company, 2003.

Shaara, Michael. *The Killer Angels*. Ballantine Book, 1974.

Shea, Christopher. *The Brawl on the Mall*. (Preservation), January/February 2001.

Sheehan, Neil. *A Bright Shining Lie*. Random House, 1988.

Sides, Hampton. *Blood and Thunder*. Doubleday. 2006.

_____. *On Desperate Ground*. Doubleday. 2018.

Thomas, Christopher A. *The Lincoln Memorial & American Life*. Princeton University Press, 2002.

Thomas, Lewis. *The Medusa and the Snail*, Penguin, 1995.

Tzu, Sun, (translated by John Minford). *The Art of War*. Penguin Books, 2002.

Veitch, Michael. *Veteran's Day*. Burt Street Music (BMI), 2011.

Waller, Douglas. *Wild Bill Donovan*. Free Press, 2011.

Whelan, Richard, *Drawing the Line*. Little Brown, 1989.

Wills, Garry. *Lincoln at Gettysburg*. Simon & Schuster, 1992.

WALLS ARISE

Walls arise—some crumble.
None are built without meaning—some without reason.

Imaginary, physical, transparent, solid, flimsy, rugged,
All are real.
In the mind, on the field, near the house, around the country.
Around me.

Built over eons,
In a moment, at the blink of an eye, the flash of a neuron.
With doors, with towers....
With spaces between—double walls.
With windows. With cracks,

Some you see. Most you can't.

Protect, divide, demark, deter, defer, demean, announce,
They become symbols of themselves ... or of something else.
Tall, veiled, broad, long,
They offer hope, safety, worship, space.
Fear.

Good. Evil. Benign.
Some fall. Some open. Some hurdled.

They tell of countries, prisons, temples, ancient cities, totalitarian states,
People.
They stand so that words or symbols or colors or scribble or paint or faces can be applied.
Faces applied.
Faces of the lost, the searching, the criminal, the loved one.
And their hopes.

The hopes and fears of those that meet at the wall,
The wall becomes the feeling of the people.
And the people become the strength of the many who overtime, each day,
come to see, to exchange, to weep, to laugh.

The Western Wall, the Walls of Jericho, the Berlin Wall, the Iron Curtain, the Great Wall of China, the Vietnam Wall.
The walls of my mind.

What is in the soul that makes them come?
What is it they need . . . the guilt, the grief, the . . . ?
Why is it always feelings of guilt or grief or despair or . . . ?

A new wall arises.
Look in my eyes. . . . Listen to my heart.

©1995 Louis Nelson

WALLS

*Music by Judy Collins, Words by Judy Collins and Louis Nelson.
Universal Music Corp. (ASCAP)/ The Wildflowers Company (ASCAP)
(Administered by Universal Music Corp.)*

We are not forgotten.
Listen to my heart, look into my eyes.
I have seen the stars falling from the skies.
Listen to my fears, yours will lift and fly.
Let me show you where, I have touched the air.
Stories from the past, each as true as mine.

We are not forgotten anymore.

These are things I know, trampled fields of snow
Sheets of falling rain, hope that conquers pain.
Souls that call again in my memory.
Through the veils of light falling on the sea.
Letters wrapped in love, lips pressed in my dreams.
Holy thoughts and brave, men who laugh and weep

We are not forgotten anymore.

I am the face on the wall,
Spirit of hope ever rising
I am the prayer in your heart for peace.

Nothing can protects us like a wall.
From our foes and our fears.
Nothing can be broken like a wall.
With our hopes and our tears

We learned all too well, hard as you may try.
There are days you win, there are days you die.
Having seen the war, we can speak of peace.
How we prayed all night for the dawn's release.
Did we all come home, did we turn the page?
There are walls of joy, there are walls of rage.
Walls at which you weep, walls on which you dance
Walls made of regret, walls you meet by chance.
Walls that break your heart, walls through which you can see.
Walls made in your mind, walls that set you free.

We are not forgotten anymore.

I am the face on the wall,
Spirit of hope ever rising
I am the prayer in your heart for peace.

©1995 Judy Collins & Louis Nelson

SUPPLEMENT

WASHINGTON POST

In July 1995, the opinion page of the *Washington Post* printed my thoughts on the occasion of the dedication of the Korean War Veterans Memorial.

REMEMBERING THE 'FORGOTTEN WAR'

We build memorials to remember those who sacrificed so much. We make pilgrimages to these memorials to search for meaning and renew our commitment to a higher purpose—to somehow resolve our inner conflicts and urge ourselves forward to find a better way . . .

The mural itself is a portrait of the common soldier . . . Caucasian, African American, Hispanic, Asian and Native American. . . . In the three neighboring monuments, war is remembered in three ways:

> *The Lincoln Memorial commemorates a great leader who led the country out of Civil War. In a universal sense, it represents all great leaders.*

> *The Vietnam Memorial mourns those who gave their lives in that dividing war. In its simplicity of design, in its honor roll of those who died, it heals and binds the shattered assumptions that changed our consciousness.*

> *The Korean Memorial remembers those who served and suggests that we not forget that complex time in history nor the personal histories of those who serve in each and every war.*

I came of age between the Korean and the Vietnam wars, and I served my country as a helicopter pilot in Germany when the Wall was being built in Berlin. Three decades later, when the Wall was dismantled, I started work on the design of the Korean Memorial. With it, a new wall arises—not one that divides, but one that will unite us.

—Louis Nelson

SUPPLEMENT

DESIGNERS OF NATIONAL MEMORIALS & MONUMENTS ON THE NATIONAL MALL. PARTIAL LIST

MEMORIAL	DEDICATED	DESIGNER/ARTIST
Washington Monument	1885	Robert Mills, Design Architect Thos. Lincoln Casey, Colonel, Corps of Engineers Chief Engineer & re-designer.
Statue of Liberty	1886	Frédéric Auguste Bartholdi, Sculptor Alexandre-Gustave Eiffel, Engineer
Gettysburg National Battleground	1895	David McConaughy, Lawyer/Planner David Wills, Lawyer/Planner William Saunders, Landscape Arch Randolph Rogers, Sculptor Caspar Buberl, Sculptor
Lincoln Memorial	1922	Daniel Chester French, Sculptor Jules Guérin, Muralist Henry Bacon, Architect
World War I Memorial	1931	Frederick H. Brooke, Architect (District of Columbia)
Jefferson Memorial	1943	Rudulph Evans, Sculptor John Russell Pope, Architect
USS Arizona Memorial Pearl Harbor Memorial	1962	Alfred Preis, Architect
Vietnam Veterans Memorial	1982	Maya Ying Lin, Designer, Memorial Frederick Hart, Sculptor Glenna Goodacre, Sculptor Cooper-Lecky, Architect-of-Record Jan C. Scruggs, Founder, Planner

MEMORIAL	DEDICATED	DESIGNER/ARTIST
Korean War Veterans Memorial	1995	Frank Gaylord, Sculptor, Memorial Louis Nelson, Designer/Artist, Mural Cooper-Lecky, Architects Gen (Ret). Richard G. Stilwell, Chair, Advisory Board
Franklin D. Roosevelt Memorial	1997	Lawrence Halpern, Designer Leonard Baskin, Artist Neil Estern, Artist Robert Graham, Sculptor Thomas Hardy, Artist George Segal, Artist
Flight 93 National Memorial Shanksville, Pennsylvania	2002	Paul Murdock, Architect
World War II Memorial	2004	Ray Kaskey, Sculptor Friedrich St. Florian, Architect
Pentagon 9/11 Memorial	2008	Julie Beckman and Keith Kaseman, Architects and Designers.
National 9/11 Memorial World Trade Center New York	2011	Michael Arad, Designer Peter Walker, Landscape Architect
Martin Luther King, Jr. Memorial	2011	Devraux and Purnell ROMA Design Group. Designers Lei Yixin, Sculptor Nicholas Benson, Inscription designer/stone carver

GLOSSARY OF ACRONYMS AND ABBREVIATIONS

ABMC	American Battle Monuments Commission
APO	Army Post Office
AT&T	American Telephone and Telegraph
B-17	A four engine WWII bomber
BL3	Winning design team of the KWVM competition
CBS	Columbia Broadcasting System
CEO	Chief Executive Office
CFA	Commission of Fine Arts
CIA	Central Intelligence Agency
D day	Battle of Normandy
DC	District of Columbia
DPRK	Democratic People's Republic of Korea (North Korea)
ERA	Equal Rights Amendment
FDA	Food and Drug Administration
FDR	Franklin Delano Roosevelt
H-13	A small bubble cockpit helicopter manufactured by Bell Helicopter
H-21	A multi seat helicopter Manufactured by Piasecki resembling a banana
H-23	A small Bubble cockpit helicopter manufactured by Hiller
H-34	An 18 passenger single rotor helicopter manufactured by Sikorsky
HU-1A	The Huey helicopter manufactured by Bell Helicopter
IBM	International Business Machines

ICTY	International Criminal Tribunal of the formal' Yugoslavia
ISIS	Islamic State of Iraq and Syria
K (klicks)	Kilometer, knot (speed or distance)
KATUSA	Korean Service Corps
KKK	Ku Klux Klan
KWVM	Korean War Veterans Memorial
NATO	North Atlantic Treaty Organization
NCPC	National Capital Planning Commission
NEA	National Endowment for the Arts
NOVA	Documentary series on science
PS	Public School
RNA	Ribonucleic acid
ROK	Republic of Korea (South Korea)
ROTC	Reserve Officers Training Corps
RPG	Rocket Propelled Grenade
(Third) 3ACR	3rd Armored Cavalry Regiment
TWA	Trans World Airlines
UK	United Kingdom
UN	United Nations
UNICEF	United Nation Children's Fund
US	United States
USNS	United States Naval Ship
VE day	Victory in Europe
VFW	Veterans of Foreign Wars
VJ day	Victory in Japan
WNYE	Call letters for New York Education radio station
WWII	World War II

Other charts and lists are not included in this list.

CITATION FOR MEDAL OF HONOR. RAYMOND G. DAVIS

Congressional Medal of Honor Society

DAVIS, RAYMOND G.
Rank: Lieutenant Colonel
Organization: U.S. Marine Corps
Company: 1st Battalion
Division: 7th Marines, 1st Marine Division
Born: 13 January 1915, Fitzgerald, Ga.
Departed: Yes
Entered Service At: Atlanta, Ga.
G.O. Number:
Date of Issue:
Accredited To:
Place / Date: Vicinity Hagaru-ri, Korea, 1 through 4 December 1950

Citation

For conspicuous gallantry and intrepidity at the risk of his life above and beyond the call of duty as commanding officer of the 1st Battalion, in action against enemy aggressor forces. Although keenly aware that the operation involved breaking through a surrounding enemy and advancing 8 miles along primitive icy trails in the bitter cold with every passage disputed by a savage and determined foe, Lt. Col. Davis boldly led his battalion into the attack in a daring attempt to relieve a beleaguered rifle company and to seize, hold, and defend a vital mountain pass controlling the only route available for 2 marine regiments in danger of being cut off by numerically superior hostile forces during their re-deployment to the port of Hungnam. When the battalion immediately encountered strong opposition from entrenched enemy forces commanding high ground in the path of the advance, he promptly spearheaded his unit in a fierce attack up the steep, ice-covered slopes in the face of withering fire and, personally leading the assault groups in a hand-to-hand encounter, drove the hostile troops from their positions, rested his men, and reconnoitered the area under enemy fire to determine the best route for continuing the mission. Always in the thick of the fighting Lt. Col. Davis led his battalion over 3 successive ridges in the deep snow in continuous attacks against the enemy and, constantly inspiring and encouraging his men throughout the night, brought his unit to a point within 1,500 yards of the surrounded rifle company by daybreak. Although knocked to the ground when a shell fragment struck his helmet and 2 bullets pierced his clothing, he arose and fought his way forward at the head of his men until he reached the isolated marines. On the following morning, he bravely led his battalion in securing the vital mountain pass from a strongly entrenched and numerically superior hostile force, carrying all his wounded with him, including 22 litter cases and numerous ambulatory patients. Despite repeated savage and heavy assaults by the enemy, he stubbornly held the vital terrain until the 2 regiments of the division had deployed through the pass and, on the morning of 4 December, led his battalion into Hagaru-ri intact. By his superb leadership, outstanding courage, and brilliant tactical ability, Lt. Col. Davis was directly instrumental in saving the beleaguered rifle company from complete annihilation and enabled the 2 marine regiments to escape possible destruction. His valiant devotion to duty and unyielding fighting spirit in the face of almost insurmountable odds enhance and sustain the highest traditions of the U.S. Naval Service.

ABOUT THE AUTHOR

Louis Nelson, an industrial designer for more than fifty years, touches our lives. He has influenced much of what we see and hear, taste and smell... how we walk and talk, learn and feel.

He has studied America's monuments and memorials for the last forty years; spent five years designing the mural at the Korean War Veterans Memorial, consulting with the sculptor and the creative team. He designed and produced the Dag Hammarskjöld Medal for the United Nations, developed designs for the World War I and the World War II Memorial in Washington, DC, the 9/11 Memorial in Manhattan and the Pentagon.

A visionary artist in diverse disciplines of strategic planning, storytelling, filmmaking, communications, graphics and industrial design; enriched by boundless curiosity and a rare sensitivity to the world around him, his career encompasses helping travelers find their way at America's leading airports; branding and identity programs for global corporations and start-ups; and product development in the fields of mass transit, museums, telecommunications, entertainment, construction and government. He originated Nutrition Facts for the FDA and America's food packages.

A visiting lecturer at Harvard University, Pratt Institute, Stockholm's Konstfack University and Seoul's Hongik University; Louis Nelson has been honored by virtually every significant design industry organization in the country and abroad, awarded Pratt Institute's Career Achievement Award, IDSA Industrial Design Excellent Award and nominee for the Smithsonian National Design Medal. All the above led him to MOSAIC, this story of War, Monuments & Mystery. He lives in New York with his wife, the noted singer, author and performer, Judy Collins.

www.louisnelson.com

A WORD ABOUT THE TYPOGRAPHY

The typefaces used in the book are Kepler, Penumbra for titling and Umbra for the title of the book. Umbra is a display face designed in 1935 by R. Hunter Middleton for Ludlow Typograph; Penumbra, an Adobe Original, designed in 1994 by Lance Hidy is a versatile display face with four styles; Kepler, another of the Adobe Original families of typefaces, was designed in-house at Adobe Systems in 1989 by Robert Slimbach. Kepler is a vast and elegant typeface family "in the tradition of classic *modern* typefaces of the 18th century."